D1365136

From the
Thomas Center
Staff 11-'93

Historic North Carolina Inns

A
Cook's Tour

by
M'Layne Murphy
and
Jill Ungerman

Photography and Art Direction
by
Kelly Harris and Jerry Price

Shearer Publishing
Fredericksburg, Texas

First published in the United States in 1989 by

Shearer Publishing
406 Post Oak Road
Fredericksburg, Texas 78624

Library of Congress Catalog Card Number — 89-061392

ISBN 0-940672-47-2

Manufactured in the United States of America
First Edition

Contents

Preface

Traveling the interstates and back roads of North Carolina in search of historic inns serving wonderful food, we discovered a state flavored with history. As we enjoyed a hearty breakfast on the Outer Banks, we were conscious that Roanoke Island, the birthplace of colonial America in 1584, was nearby. In the high country we were served Southern favorites based on traditional recipes, with some of the oldest mountains in the world right out the kitchen doorstep.

North Carolina, from the sandy dunes of the coast to the snow-capped mountains of the west, is as varied as the food we sampled. Whether we were savoring house specialties, served family-style in the dining room of a former turn-of-the-century farmstead, or feasting on French-inspired cuisine in a historic restaurant with an international reputation, we found the chefs shared a common dedication to serving only the best.

Most of the recipes appearing in this book are usually prepared in large quantities and in professionally staffed kitchens. To assist the reader, we asked the chefs to provide helpful tips for preparing their recipes at home—these are the "Chef's Tips." The recipes of each inn we visited have been tested for the home kitchen. In our testing and tasting we also took careful note of any information that might be beneficial to the reader—these are included as "Tips."

No inn paid to be included in this book. They did contribute valuable time and information to the project. Along with an introduction to each inn you will find a phone number and address for obtaining specific information on rates and accommodations. Most of the inns are usually booked far in advance, so we recommend making reservations well ahead of your arrival.

Take your own tour and discover North Carolina for yourself. Waiting to share the histories of their inns and their own versions of Southern hospitality are the gracious innkeepers and chefs who made our cook's tour memorable.

Acknowledgments

Special thanks to the innkeepers and chefs who shared their recipes and answered our many questions during the testing of these recipes.

Grateful acknowledgment is also made to the following: Cataloochee Ranch, information and recipes, pages 100 to 106, from *Catalooche Cooking*, published by Cataloochee Ranch, Route 1, Box 500F, Maggie Valley, North Carolina, 28751. Fryemont Inn, Bryson City, North Carolina: photo, page 107. Fearrington House Restaurant and Country Inn, Pittsboro, North Carolina: photos, pages 37, 38, 39, 40, and 47; recipes, pages 39, 40, 41, 43, 44, 45, 46, and 47 from *The Fearrington House Cookbook* by Jenny Fitch, published by Ventana Press, Inc., P. O. Box 2468, Chapel Hill, North Carolina 27515.

Our special appreciation to Judith Hipskind Collins and Burt Oelker for their comments and suggestions on our project.

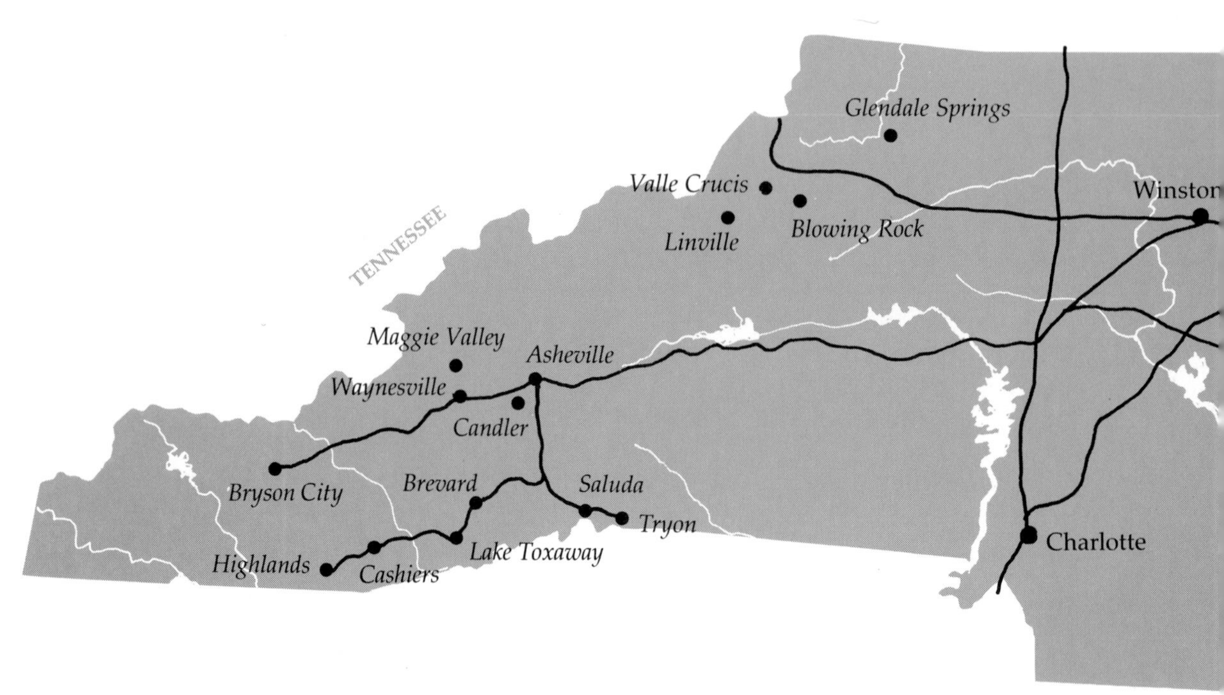

North Carolina

Shown on this map of North Carolina are the locations of the historic inns included in this "cook's tour" as well as major cities as reference points. The addresses and phone numbers of each inn are provided at the end of their respective section for your convenience. It is recommended that you contact each inn for current room status, rates, and specific directions. Most inns have brochures listing area activities, points of interest, seasonal events, and dining arrangements.

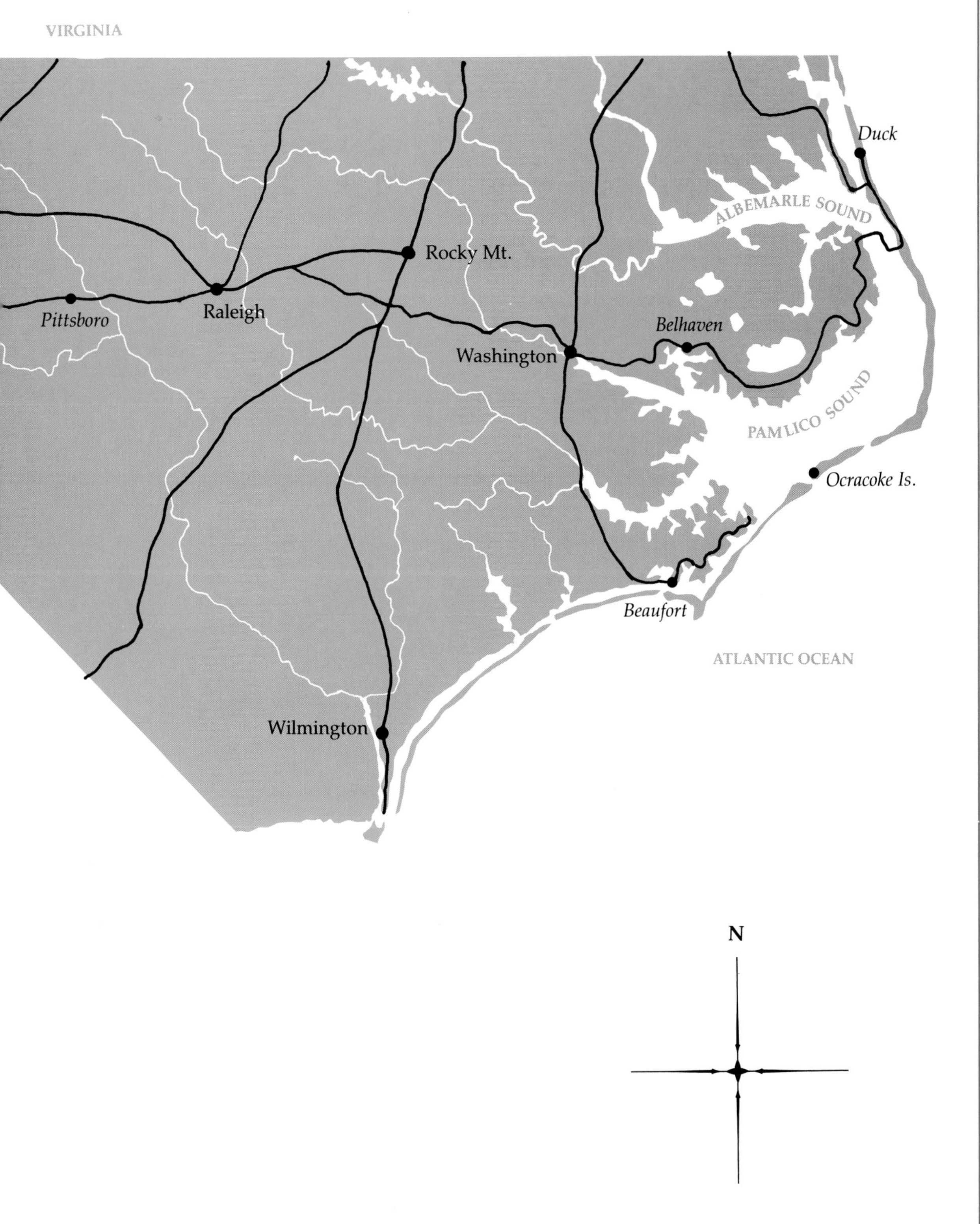
VIRGINIA
Duck
ALBEMARLE SOUND
Rocky Mt.
Pittsboro
Raleigh
Belhaven
Washington
PAMLICO SOUND
Ocracoke Is.
Beaufort
ATLANTIC OCEAN
Wilmington
N

The Sanderling Inn and Restaurant

Melting glaciers from the last ice age formed a series of low-lying barrier islands and peninsulas off the coast of North Carolina. Called the Outer Banks, these undulating sands with their haunting beauty captivated the earliest visitors.

Exploring for France in 1524, the Florentine navigator Giovanni da Verranzano reported his enchantment with this "pleasant and delectable" land and inspired Sir Walter Raleigh's scouting expedition for England. Raleigh sent colonists to establish the "New Empire" on Roanoke Island in 1587, but after returning from a trip home for supplies, Captain John White found that the colony had disappeared completely.

Up and down the coast are many points of historic interest: Nags Head, where lantern-carrying horses walked on the beaches to suggest anchored ships, luring real ships so close to shore that they were easy plunder; Kill Devil Hills, where locals loved a New England rum so powerful it could "kill the devil"; Cape Hatteras of hurricane fame; and Kitty Hawk, where the Wright brothers made their flights in 1903.

Surrounded by unspoiled beaches and sea-grass-covered sand dunes of the remote northern banks is the Sanderling Inn and Restaurant.

The restaurant building, originally built in 1899 as Caffey's Inlet U.S. Lifesaving Station No. 5, was one of the initial seven stations built for surfmen who rescued shipwrecked passengers and crew. Over 500 ships—from pirate schooners to German submarines—are reportedly beneath the turbulent currents of the 110-mile coast.

Listed on the National Register of Historic Landmarks, the station has been tastefully and faithfully restored to preserve its maritime character. Inside, a series of dining rooms, meeting rooms, and lounges all boast spectacular views. Under the direction of twenty-two-year-old executive chef Marvin Herrera, the Sanderling Restaurant is known for its hickory-grilled dishes plus staff interpretations of local cuisine. The restaurant prepares early breakfasts and sack lunches for avid anglers and birdwatchers.

The inn itself, with twenty-eight rooms and loft suites, which are of new construction, was designed to meet stringent regional architectural criteria. Each room offers private porches that open to the sun and views of the ocean, Currituck Sound, or sand dunes.

The two-and-a-half-story main lobby, of polished pine from floor to ceiling, houses an impressive collection of Boehm birds and Royal Worcester fish. Upstairs, a library filled with books and periodicals features an elephant folio edition of Audubon prints in four massive leather-bound volumes. From the main lobby a decked patio reaches out over the sands and overlooks the sound.

Guests also enjoy membership privileges at the golf and tennis club, which is part of this resort-residential community, developed and owned by Earl Slick, a Winston-Salem businessman. And within minutes there is reportedly some of the best surf fishing on the East Coast, plus hang gliding, wind surfing, kiting, scuba diving, hunting, and the 3,400-acre Pine Island Audubon Sanctuary, where hundreds of species of birds and other wildlife are protected in their natural environment.

The Sanderling Inn and Restaurant, a civilized oasis in this wilderness, offers the benefits of a classic seaside resort—right down to the hand-written weather report left on your pillow each evening.

Hickory-Grilled Barbecue Shrimp

Serves 2 to 4

Tip: Serves 2 for dinner, 4 as an appetizer.

Tip: We used the large 8- to 10-count shrimp. Adjust bacon according to the number of shrimp per pound.

Chef's tip: Chef Marvin Herrera makes his popular barbecue dishes by starting with a good commercial barbecue sauce. Then he adds molasses, brown sugar, and vinegar to suit the particular dish he is preparing.

1 pound shrimp
8 strips bacon
barbecue sauce

Boil shrimp for 3 minutes. Peel, devein, and wrap in bacon strip, securing with a toothpick. Dip shrimp in barbecue sauce and grill 3 to 4 minutes. Serve immediately.

Sweet Potato Vichyssoise

Serves 8 to 10

4 medium sweet potatoes, peeled and thinly sliced
1 medium onion, coarsely chopped
3 pints (6 cups) chicken broth
½ teaspoon ground cinnamon
½ teaspoon ground allspice
¼ teaspoon ground ginger
1 quart (4 cups) heavy cream

Simmer all ingredients, except heavy cream, until potatoes are soft. Put through a food processor or blender while adding the heavy cream. Chill thoroughly and serve in chilled bowls.

Wild Mushroom Bisque

Serves 8

1 pound wild mushrooms
1 pound (4 sticks) butter
1 cup flour
1 gallon (16 cups) chicken stock
1 pint (2 cups) half-and-half

Process mushrooms in a food processor for 1 minute. Melt the butter in a large saucepan, add mushrooms, and cook for 6 to 7 minutes. Add flour, stirring constantly, and continue cooking for 8 minutes. Add the chicken stock and cook slowly until heated. Add the half-and-half, mix well, and serve.

Tip: The wild mushrooms give this bisque a wonderful and distinctive flavor, but regular mushrooms can be used with successful results.

Tip: Do not allow mixture to come to a hard boil or bisque will thin and separate.

Pan-Fried Chicken

Serves 4

2 chickens
1 cup milk
2 cups flour
1 tablespoon salt
1 tablespoon cayenne pepper
1 tablespoon black pepper
1 tablespoon paprika
½ cup oil

Preheat oven to 350 degrees.

Remove breasts and legs from chicken and debone. Dip chicken pieces in milk. Mix flour with seasonings. Dredge chicken in flour mixture and fry in the oil heated to 325 degrees. Fry until golden brown. Drain chicken and finish cooking in oven for 7 minutes. Serve immediately.

Tip: Breast and leg pieces can be substituted for the whole chickens. If using whole chickens, reserve remaining parts for other purposes.

Fricassee of Scallops, Shrimp, Oysters, and Blue Crab

Serves 4 to 6

Tip: The Sanderling Inn Restaurant serves 4 with this recipe. We found it could easily serve 8.

12 large shrimp, peeled and deveined
16 large sea scallops
2 pints (4 cups) water
4 ounces shallots, minced
white pepper, salt, and sugar to taste
1 pint (2 cups) heavy cream
24 ounces fettuccine, cooked
16 oysters, shucked and drained
8 ounces jumbo lump crabmeat

Tip: We first boiled the shrimp shells in the water, strained it, then used it to parboil the shrimp and scallops.

In a large sauté pan or frying pan place the shrimp, scallops, water, shallots, and seasonings. Bring to a boil, stirring frequently, then simmer until shrimp begins to turn pink and become slightly firmer. Remove shrimp and scallops and set aside.

Chef's tip: This method of reducing the sauce allows the natural flavors of the seafood to intensify.

Gently boil stock until it is reduced in volume by half. Add heavy cream and cook until mixture begins to thicken, stirring frequently.

Add fettuccine and continue cooking over a high heat until sauce reaches a nice thickness, tossing frequently. Add shrimp, scallops, and oysters and toss with fettuccine. Add the crabmeat and toss for another 30 seconds. Serve immediately with a green salad.

Sweet Potato Pecan Pie

Yields one 10-inch pie

½ cup pecans, chopped
2 teaspoons butter
¾ cup brown sugar
10-inch pie shell, unbaked
14-ounce can sweet potatoes or yams
1 teaspoon ginger
¼ teaspoon powdered cloves
1½ teaspoons cinnamon
¼ teaspoon salt
2 eggs, beaten
1½ cups milk

Preheat oven to 350 degrees.

Combine pecans, butter, and brown sugar in a saucepan and heat to 450 degrees, using a candy thermometer and stirring constantly. Spread into a prepared pie shell and bake for 10 minutes. Remove from oven and cool.

Beat sweet potatoes until smooth and add remaining ingredients, again beating until smooth. Pour into cooled pie shell and bake about 45 minutes or until spatula inserted an inch from the edge comes out clean. Cool before serving.

Honey-Vanilla Ice Cream

Yields approximately ½ gallon

8 egg yolks
1½ quarts (6 cups) half-and-half
½ cup honey
1 cup sugar
3 tablespoons vanilla
3 cups (1½ pints) heavy cream

Blend all ingredients except heavy cream and heat in a double boiler or water bath for 30 minutes or until mixture coats a spoon. Chill. Add 3 cups of heavy cream to chilled mixture. Process in any type of ice cream maker. Freeze and serve.

Tip: To make a water bath, boil a pan of water and place pan containing ice cream ingredients in water.

Triple Chocolate Mousse Cake

Yields one 9-inch four-layer cake

6 ounces semisweet chocolate
1¾ ounces baker's chocolate
½ cup (1 stick) margarine
1½ cups sugar
2 eggs
¾ cup buttermilk
1 teaspoon vanilla
1 teaspoon baking soda
1⅓ cups flour
1 tablespoon cornstarch

Filling

2 ounces semisweet chocolate
3 eggs
6 egg yolks
2½ cups (1¼ pints) heavy cream
½ cup confectioners' sugar
6 egg whites

Icing

4 ounces semisweet chocolate
1 teaspoon vegetable oil
1 cup (½ pint) heavy cream
1 cup toasted coconut (optional)

Preheat oven to 350 degrees.

To make cake, melt both kinds of chocolate together in a double boiler and set aside.

Cream margarine and sugar; add eggs, buttermilk, and vanilla. Mix well.

Combine all dry ingredients, then add to mixture of wet ingredients. Add melted chocolate. Mix well. Pour into two well-greased and floured 9-inch cake pans. Bake for about 30 minutes or until done. Remove layers from pans and cool on racks.

To prepare filling, melt chocolate in a double boiler and then cool. Add whole eggs and mix well. Add egg yolks and mix well. Set aside.

Whip cream to soft peaks, add sugar slowly, and continue beating until peaks become slightly stiffer.

Whip egg whites to stiff but not dry peaks. In a separate bowl combine small amounts of the whipped cream mixture and the egg whites. Then add remaining whipped cream mixture and the egg whites, folding together carefully. Fold in melted chocolate and set aside.

To assemble cake, trim cake layers, removing any overly moist or bulging surfaces. Slice each cake layer into two layers. Place one layer in the bottom of a 9-inch springform pan. Spread with ⅓ of the mousse mixture and cover with second layer. Spread with ⅓ more of the mousse mixture and cover with third layer. Add the rest of the mousse and top with the final layer. Chill cake for one hour or until ready to serve.

To make icing, melt chocolate in a double boiler and remove from heat. Blend in heavy cream and oil.

Remove cake from pan and place on a wire rack. Pour icing over cake, smoothing top with metal spatula and letting excess drip down the sides. Coat sides with toasted coconut if desired.

Chef's tip: Keep cake refrigerated.

The Sanderling Inn and Restaurant
S.R. Box 319Y, Duck
Kitty Hawk,
North Carolina 27949
919-261-4111

General Manager:
Stephen J. Berger

Island Inn and Restaurant

As the ferry pushed off at Swan Quarter, no destination came to view. The trip across thirty-mile-wide Pamlico Sound required almost three hours by the auto and passenger ferry, which makes two scheduled daily runs. Incredible as it may seem, unless you have your own plane, the ferry is the fastest way to get to Ocracoke. No wonder its island inhabitants were isolated from the rest of the world for 200 years—until 1960, when the ferry began regular service.

As a result of this isolation, the islanders have retained their English-sounding accent. Most of the 660 residents believe they are descendants of merchants from Devon or from the 400 followers of Edward Teach, better known as Blackbeard, who originally sailed from Bristol.

In fact, Ocracoke was once headquarters of Blackbeard and his fleet of four pirate ships. According to local legend, one of the first things Teach did after setting up his "business" was to change the name Pilot Town to something zippier. Seeing the sixteen-mile stretch of white sand, he is said to have cried, "Oh, crow cock!"—thus giving the island its name.

Small clapboard cottages with picket-fenced yards line the narrow dirt roads. Thanks to the warmth of the Gulf Stream current, an abundance of southern flora—including gardenias, mimosa, yaupon tea bushes, and yucca—fill the yards with color.

At the southern end of the village, basking white in the warm sun, lies the Island Inn and Restaurant. Built in 1901, the inn remains the longest continuously operating inn of the region.

The owners of the inn, Foy Shaw and Larry Williams, work to preserve the natural beauty of the island as well as the historic integrity of their inn. The two owners, along with most of the island residents, were responsible for passage of a law prohibiting future high-rise development.

Many of the rooms in the main building have recently undergone major changes. The eagle's nest loft suite of polished woods and uncluttered elegance became the prototype for future restorations. The inn has more casual accommodations in a separate building beside the only heated pool on Ocracoke.

The dining room is under the separate ownership of Theotis Brooks and Chester Lynn. Chester has worked at the inn since he was ten; his mother did the cooking before him for almost seventeen years. Both he and Theotis take pride in creating recipes using ingredients from the waters around Ocracoke. Their versions of East Coast favorites such as clam chowder and crab cakes are especially good and exceptionally easy to prepare.

The most famous inhabitants of Ocracoke are the blue crabs, whose yearly molt is cause for celebration. Beginning in early May, an annual crab fest features two tons of soft-shell crabs and slaw, a ten-kilometer crab race, and the selection of a "crab princess."

Three public routes will lead you out of Ocracoke—back by the Swan Quarter ferry, a ferry to Cedar Island, or all the way up North Carolina Highway 12. The highway offers the opportunity to visit the many historic landmarks of the region, to sit on the glistening white sands and sunbathe, to bird-watch, to fish, or just to contemplate the bounty of the Outer Banks.

Ocracoke Clam Chowder

Serves 6

4 ounces salt pork, washed and diced
1 small onion, chopped
4 cups chicken stock
4 potatoes, diced
1 pint clams, chopped, with juice
½ teaspoon Old Bay Seafood Seasoning
black pepper to taste

Fry salt pork in a heavy pot. When salt pork is brown, add the onion, stirring occasionally until onions are cooked. Add chicken stock and bring to a boil. Add potatoes and simmer until potatoes are cooked. Add clams, juice, and seasonings. Bring to a boil, reduce heat, and simmer for 10 minutes. Serve immediately.

Crab Cakes

Yields 12 large cakes

2 pounds lump crabmeat
½ cup onion, chopped
½ teaspoon Old Bay Seafood Seasoning
2 eggs, beaten
1 teaspoon dry mustard
3 tablespoons mayonnaise
1 teaspoon parsley flakes
1 cup bread crumbs
oil for frying
lemon wedges

Mix all ingredients, adding bread crumbs last. Pat into small cakes and fry until done and lightly browned on both sides. Serve immediately with lemon wedges if desired.

Fish Cakes

Yields 25 to 30 portions

5 pounds fish (any variety), boiled
1 onion, finely chopped
2 stalks celery, finely chopped
12 eggs
6 tablespoons parsley flakes
dash of Old Bay Seafood Seasoning
salt and pepper to taste
2 cups or more bread crumbs
oil for frying (optional)
lemon wedges

Drain fish and let cool. Mix onion, celery, eggs, and seasonings with boiled fish. Work together until mixed well.

Add bread crumbs until mixture will hold together. Pat into cakes. Grill or deep-fry. Serve immediately with lemon wedges.

Tip: This recipe can be cut proportionately to 1 pound of fish with excellent results.

Clam Fritters

Serves 4

1 pint clams, chopped
2 eggs, beaten
1 small onion, minced
2 tablespoons flour
salt and pepper to taste
4 tablespoons oil
lemon wedges

Mix ingredients together in order listed. Heat oil in frying pan. Spoon mixture into the hot oil, forming small cakes. Brown on both sides. Serve immediately with lemon wedges if desired.

Tip: If egg runs slightly, scrape back toward center of fritter with a spatula.

Fig Cake

Yields one tube cake

3 eggs
1½ cups sugar
1 cup oil
2 cups flour
1 teaspoon nutmeg
1 teaspoon allspice
1 teaspoon cinnamon
1 teaspoon salt
1 teaspoon baking soda, dissolved in a little hot water
½ cup buttermilk
1 teaspoon vanilla
1 cup preserved figs, chopped
1 cup nuts, chopped

Glaze

¼ cup buttermilk
½ cup sugar
¼ teaspoon baking soda
1½ teaspoons cornstarch
¼ cup (½ stick) butter or margarine
1½ teaspoons vanilla

Preheat oven to 350 degrees.

Beat eggs, add sugar and oil. Sift all dry ingredients together. Add to egg mixture, alternating with buttermilk. Add vanilla; fold in figs and nuts. Pour into a greased tube or oblong pan and bake until done—about 45 minutes.

To make glaze, combine all ingredients except vanilla in a saucepan and bring to a boil. Remove from heat and cool. Slowly add vanilla. Spoon over warm cake and serve.

Tip: This cake was much better than expected. Moist, light, and delicate in flavor, it is not too sweet to serve for breakfast.

Tip: You can spoon any leftover sauce directly onto the slices of cake with delicious results.

Howardy Cake

Yields one oblong or tube cake

¾ cup (1½ sticks) margarine, softened
2 cups sugar
3 cups flour
2 teaspoons baking soda
6 tablespoons cocoa
1 teaspoon salt
2 tablespoons vinegar
2 cups water

Preheat oven to 350 degrees.

Cream together margarine and sugar. Sift together remaining dry ingredients and combine with margarine mixture and liquids. Pour batter into a greased, floured tube pan or 9- × 13-inch oblong baking pan. Bake for 25 to 35 minutes or until done. Serve warm or cold.

Note: This is a simple, excellent cake, similar to a chocolate pound cake.

Island Inn and Restaurant
P.O. Box 9
Ocracoke Island, North Carolina 27960
919-928-4351

Innkeepers: Foy Shaw and Larry Williams
Restaurant Owners: Theotis Brooks and Chester Lynn

River Forest Manor

Way off the beaten path by land but long a familiar landmark to yachtsmen sailing the Intercoastal Waterway, River Forest Manor gleamed starkly white as the first traces of the full moon rose behind this glorious old Southern mansion. Light-filled windows greeted visitors from land or by sea.

Belhaven itself, especially by night, seemed as peaceful as it must have been in 1899 when construction began on the original structure. Only the sleek yachts in the bay and the private planes on the landing field pierced the time warp we felt we had suddenly entered. Inside were reminders of an elegant past. Ornate ceilings and oak mantles of the eleven fireplaces carved by Italian artisans remain beautifully preserved. The lobby, paneled in Honduras mahogany, houses technological relics, memorabilia, and art. The ladies' room is also something of a museum with a gigantic sleigh bed as its main attraction. A stranded visitor that night was allowed to use it once all the dinner guests had left for the evening.

Axson Smith bought and converted the old mansion in 1947. Through the years River Forest Manor has attracted a celebrity clientele, including James Cagney, Tallulah Bankhead, Burl Ives, and Walter Cronkite. Today, Melba Smith and her two sons, Axson and Mark, operate the inn, restaurant, and dock facilities.

Although we must admit to being less than enthusiastic about smorgasbord-style dining, we were delightfully surprised. Yes, you do put together your own salad, but here were such wonderful morsels as freshly pickled sunchokes, watermelon-rind pickles, and headcheese. River Forest Manor has three chefs who have been cooking for the inn for a minimum of fifteen years each. When sunchoke season comes around, the pantry is stocked with pickles. This is true for watermelon and other seasonable foods.

The chefs also prepare a wonderful sausage right at the inn. Melba Smith took us to a room that was festooned—from window to window, from chair to chair—with plump, pale pink sausages. Fans blew on them from all directions. Three to five hundred pounds of sausage are prepared at one time. Half is frozen for breakfast frying. The rest is fan-dried for pickling. This pickle recipe, like all the recipes we received from Mrs. Smith, seemed too simple, fast, and good to be true.

As we departed the next morning, the entire exterior of the inn was being scrubbed down with soap and water—a frequent task that not only keeps the exterior clean but also preserves the paint in this coastal environment. And preservation is foremost with the Smiths. About ten years ago the inn's massive columns began to deteriorate. After a story about the columns ran in the local paper, Mrs. Smith received a letter from an Austrian immigrant who professed exceptional skill at reconstruction. Mrs. Smith moved him and his wife to Belhaven, where he spent the next two years completely restoring the columns, composed of small interlocking pieces of wood, as well as the foundation and the porch that gracefully surrounds this lovely North Carolina landmark.

This same care and consideration seems to be offered to every guest at River Forest Manor, whether you've wandered in unexpectedly, as we did, or whether you're a "regular" who is met by the staff at the dock and whisked away in a golf cart to this easier, quieter, more gracious time and place.

Marinated Shrimp

Serves 2 to 4

2 tablespoons vinegar
1 tablespoon lemon juice
3 tablespoons vegetable oil
1 teapoon dry mustard
salt to taste
½ pound shrimp, boiled, peeled, and deveined
1 medium onion, finely chopped
1 small green pepper, chopped
1 stalk celery, chopped

Combine all ingredients and refrigerate for 3 hours. Serve as an appetizer or party dish.

Note: This is one of Melba Smith's personal favorites.

Tip: As with most of the River Forest Manor recipes, which are served primarily smorgasbord-style, the number of servings per recipe can vary. Most would be excellent for a party buffet. Increasing this recipe is also easy.

Pickled Sausage

Serves 2 to 6

1 pound all-pork link sausage, air-dried
1 cup vinegar
1 cup water

Cut sausage into 1½-inch pieces. Place in skillet and cover with vinegar and water. Cook covered over medium heat until sausage is well done, about 1½ hours. Serve with sour sauce from skillet.

Note: This simple but loved recipe was developed by Axson Smith and has been served for over thirty-seven years. Some people like to make an entire meal of this sausage.

Tip: Good link sausage can be dried overnight by hanging links across two chairs and allowing a fan to blow on them.

Chef's tip: This sausage is best as an appetizer or buffet dish.

Belhaven Crab Casserole

Serves 4

1 pound fresh crabmeat
2 tablespoons onion, grated
½ cup celery, chopped
½ cup green pepper, chopped
1 cup unseasoned croutons
½ teaspoon seasoned salt
dash of hot pepper sauce
1 lemon, juiced
1 cup mayonnaise
2 tablespoons Dijon mustard
½ cup bread crumbs
2 tablespoons butter

Preheat oven to 325 degrees.

Flake crabmeat and pick through for any shells. Add onion, celery, green pepper, croutons, salt, and pepper sauce. Mix well. Mix Dijon mustard, mayonnaise, and lemon juice and add to crabmeat mixture. Spread evenly into a greased baking dish. Sprinkle with bread crumbs and dot with small squares of butter. Bake about 40 minutes or until brown and crisp on top. Serve immediately.

Oyster Fritters

Serves 2 to 4

Chef's tip: If no oyster liquid is available or if a thinner batter is desired, use a little milk.

1 pint oysters, drained and chopped
2 eggs, beaten
½ cup self-rising flour
salt and pepper to taste
oil for frying
lemon wedges

Chef's tip: These fritters are especially good if served right from the pan.

Reserve any liquid from oysters. Make a batter of oysters, eggs, flour, salt, pepper, and oyster liquid.

Heat ¾ inch of oil in frying pan. Drop batter into hot oil using large spoon. Cook until brown on one side, turn, and brown on the other. Drain on paper towels and serve immediately with lemon wedges or red seafood sauce.

Sweet Potatoes Supreme

Serves 4 to 6

Chef's tip: Also try frying peeled and sliced sweet potatoes.

4 cups (2 large) sweet potatoes, cooked and mashed
½ cup sugar
2 eggs, beaten
½ cup evaporated milk
4 tablespoons (½ stick) margarine or butter

Topping

1 cup brown sugar
½ cup (1 stick) margarine or butter
⅓ cup flour
1 cup pecans, chopped
salt to taste

Preheat oven to 350 degrees.

Combine all the ingredients for the sweet potato mixture and pour into a greased baking dish.

Combine topping ingredients and spread over sweet potatoes. Bake 30 to 40 minutes or until topping bubbles and is slightly brown. Serve immediately.

Collards

Serves 6 to 8

Chef's tip: Probably everyone in the South knows how to cook collards, but just in case, this is the real North Carolina version.

Tip: Be sure to wash salt pork before boiling. Even then, it provided enough salt for our taste.

½ pound salt pork, sliced
1 gallon water
2 pounds collard greens
salt to taste

Boil salt pork in water about 30 minutes. Wash collards twice to remove all sand. Add collards to water and cook at low boil until tender, or soft enough to mash—about 2 hours. Drain, salt to taste, and serve.

Corn Bread

Yields one 10-inch-square pan

1 cup cornmeal
⅔ cup flour
2 teaspoons baking powder
1 teaspoon salt
⅓ to ½ cup sugar
⅔ cup oil
2 eggs, beaten
1 cup milk
⅔ cup sour cream or 2 cups buttermilk
2 to 4 tablespoons extra oil

Preheat oven to 400 degrees.

Combine cornmeal, flour, baking powder, salt, sugar, oil, and eggs. Add ½ cup milk and mix well. Add remaining milk and sour cream or buttermilk. Blend well. Pour ⅓ cup oil in a 10- × 10-inch pan, then add cornmeal mixture. Spoon extra oil on top and bake about 30 minutes or until done. Cut into squares and serve immediately.

Chef's tip: Corn bread is done when top is golden and mixture pulls away from sides of pan.

Cranberry-Apple Casserole

Serves 6 to 8

3 cups apples, peeled, cored, and chopped
2 cups cranberries plus a few reserved for garnish
2 tablespoons flour
1 cup granulated sugar

Topping

1 cup pecans, chopped, plus halves reserved for garnish
½ cup brown sugar
½ cup flour
½ cup (1 stick) butter, melted

Preheat oven to 325 degrees.

Combine apples and cranberries; toss with flour and sugar. Spoon into a greased baking dish.

To prepare topping, mix pecans, brown sugar, flour, and butter. Spoon onto apple-cranberry mixture. Garnish with pecan halves and berries. Bake for 30 to 40 minutes. Serve immediately.

Note: This recipe is excellent with turkey, chicken, or pork. One guest liked it so much he put an extra serving on top of his pie.

River Forest Manor
Belhaven, North Carolina 27810
919-943-2151

Innkeepers: Melba Smith, Axson Smith, Jr., and Mark Smith

The Cedars at Beaufort

Time stands still in the small fishing village of Beaufort, where the historic inn known as the Cedars at Beaufort commands a wonderful view of the waterfront.

Today most people associate seacoast towns with high-rise condos and developments and row after row of tourist shops. This is not the case with Beaufort. Locals say its inaccessibility in the early years kept this town from becoming commercialized. Until 1926 there was no highway bridge, so travelers came by boat. Today they still come by boats and yachts from as far away as Maine and the Caribbean.

Bill and Pat Kwaak did not arrive by boat, even though the former New Jersey residents are boating enthusiasts. Bill, a retired veterinarian, and his wife were on a car trip to look for interesting marinas. What they found was an inn for sale. Years before, when first married, they discussed the possibility of someday owning an inn in Vermont or New Hampshire. After a stay at the Cedars, they quickly made a decision—perhaps a romantic one, according to Bill—to purchase the Cedars at Beaufort.

Fortunately for the Kwaaks, major restoration had been completed in 1985 by former owners, Peter and Suzin Osburn. The main building, dating from about 1768, is named the Borden House. It was built by William Borden, Jr., whose father, a Quaker, came to North Carolina in 1732. One of the interesting features of the house is the door leading to the attic. The door, which predates the house, is called a "spirit" door because its design suggests a cross and open Bible.

Shrubs and trees indigenous to the coast have been planted on the grounds as well as hundreds of flowers and herbs that were common in the Bordens' day. The accommodations in the Borden House and the historic house next door are tastefully furnished with antiques.

The talented young chef is Jonathan Osburn, son of the prior owners. His fare includes pastas, marvelous pâtés, and desserts and breads made from scratch.

There are complimentary ferry rides for inn guests to Carrot Island, just five minutes away, where herds of wild horses roam and over a hundred species of birds make their home. Another ferry destination is Shackleford Banks with its sandy beaches for swimming and shelling.

Beaufort, once a stopover, has become a vacation retreat. Landlubbers and sailors alike are intrigued by the Maritime Museum. More than a hundred eighteenth- and nineteenth-century homes line the narrow streets. The oldest home is thought to have been built by the famous pirate Blackbeard. If you elect to tour the Old Burying Ground, be sure to take along a brochure. You will be fascinated by the stories of the tombstones.

Beaufort—with its uncrowded boardwalks, nautical flags waving in the sea breeze, and gulls standing watch on the weathered pilings—is a beautiful sight. The Kwaaks' decision to make Beaufort their home is not difficult to understand.

Crab, Shrimp, and Oyster Bisque

Serves 8

1½ quarts White Fish Fumet or bottled clam juice
2 cups dry white wine
1 recipe Light Roux
½ pound back-fin crabmeat, picked to remove shells
½ pound small shrimp, peeled and deveined
3 cups heavy cream
24 oysters, shucked (reserve liquid)
salt and fresh-ground pepper to taste
1½ teaspoons fresh thyme, chopped for garnish

White Fish Fumet

Tip: Fish bones can sometimes be obtained at the fresh fish market at no charge. If bones are not available, use approximately 1 pound of white fish fillets.

4 pounds fish bones without heads
2 quarts water
2 cups white wine
8 ribs celery, coarsely chopped
2 onions, peeled and coarsely chopped
2 leeks, coarsely chopped
10 black peppercorns
4 sprigs parsley
1 tablespoon dried thyme
1 bay leaf
1 teaspoon fennel seeds
reserved liquid from oysters if available

Light Roux

½ cup (1 stick) plus 2 tablespoons unsalted butter
½ cup all-purpose flour

To prepare White Fish Fumet, combine all ingredients in a stockpot. Bring to a boil, skimming top. Simmer for 20 to 30 minutes. Strain through double thickness of cheesecloth. Set aside.

To prepare Light Roux, melt butter in a heavy-bottomed saucepan. Add flour and cook slowly over low heat, stirring constantly until light golden brown or until flour loses its raw taste. Set aside.

To prepare bisque, bring fish fumet and wine to a boil and slowly add roux, whisking until smooth. Add crabmeat and shrimp. Simmer until shrimp are cooked—about 3 minutes. Stir in heavy cream and bring back to simmer. Add oysters and cook until their edges curl—about 1 minute. Serve in warm soup plates garnished with thyme.

Chef's tip: To spice up the bisque, add 2 tablespoons cajun spice after roux is mixed in. Beware of adding too much salt.

Chef's tip: The bisque base without cream and oysters can be kept for two or three days in the refrigerator. It also freezes well.

Snapper in Almond Crust
with Lemon Beurre Blanc

Serves 4

4 6-ounce snapper fillets
1½ cups fresh bread crumbs
1½ cups almonds, blanched and sliced
½ cup all-purpose flour
2 eggs, beaten with a little water
4 tablespoons (½ stick) unsalted butter

Chef's tip: We prefer true American red snapper when available.

Lemon Beurre Blanc

3 lemons, juiced
1 small shallot, minced
¼ cup dry white wine
6 tablespoons very cold unsalted butter

Preheat oven to 450 degrees.

Process bread crumbs and almonds until the almonds are finely chopped; set aside. Dredge fillets in flour, shaking to remove excess. Dredge in egg mixture and then in crumb mixture. Make sure to coat the entire fillet evenly.

Chef's tip: The fish can be breaded several hours ahead of time, which will make it crunchier. Keep refrigerated until ready to use.

In a large ovenproof skillet, melt butter. As soon as the foam subsides, place fish in pan, lightly browning on both sides. Place fish in oven and bake for 4 to 6 minutes.

To prepare Lemon Beurre Blanc, combine lemon, shallot, and wine in a small saucepan. Reduce by three-fourths or until almost thick and syrupy. Remove from heat and beat in butter one tablespoon at a time. Sauce will thicken.

Serve fish with a little of the sauce and pass the remainder on the side.

Pan-Roasted Quail
with Calvados and Green Apples

Serves 4

Chef's tip: Quail can be purchased partially boned.

8 quail, partially boned
1 cup all-purpose flour, seasoned with salt and pepper
2 tablespoons unsalted butter
2 tablespoons peanut oil

Sauce

Chef's tip: Store sliced apples in water with a little lemon juice to prevent them from turning brown.

3 ounces Calvados (French apple brandy)
2 large green apples, thinly sliced
1 tablespoon fresh thyme, finely chopped
½ cup applesauce
1 cup chicken stock, reduced by half
salt and freshly ground black pepper to taste
green apple slices for garnish

Dredge quail in seasoned flour. Melt butter in sauté pan, add oil, and heat. When foam subsides, add quail and brown on both sides. Lower heat and cook 3 to 5 minutes or until thoroughly cooked. Remove to heated platter and keep warm during sauce preparation.

To prepare sauce, pour off all but one tablespoon of browning fat. Deglaze pan juices with Calvados, stirring and bringing to a boil. Add apples, thyme, applesauce, and chicken stock. Cook until sauce coats back of spoon—about 3 minutes. Season to taste.

Chef's tip: If it is very hot in the kitchen, have someone else taste for salt.

Serve quail with sauce spooned over and garnished with apple slices.

Apple Crème Pâtissière

Serves 8

8 large apples, cored and peeled (any variety)
1 cup sugar
2-inch stick of cinnamon
4 whole cloves
10 black peppercorns
4 whole allspice berries
1 quart dry white wine

Crème Pâtissière

½ cup sugar
3 egg yolks
⅓ cup all-purpose flour, sifted
1 cup milk, scalded
1½ teaspoons unsalted butter
2¼ teaspoons vanilla

Caramel Sauce

¼ cup water
½ cup sugar
3 egg yolks, beaten
1 cup (½ pint) heavy cream
½ tablespoon dry white wine
fresh raspberries and mint leaves for garnish

Combine sugar, spices, and wine in a medium saucepan and bring to a boil. Add apples and reduce heat. Simmer for 20 minutes or until apples are easily pierced with a knife. Remove apples from liquid and cool.

Chef's tip: If you are short of time, prepare apples or pears as above and serve with zabaglione.

To prepare Crème Pâtissière, in a large, heavy-bottomed saucepan combine sugar and egg yolks and beat until the mixture forms a ribbon. Beat in the flour. Continue beating the egg mixture while adding the milk in a slow stream. Cook over medium heat for 2 or 3 minutes while stirring briskly. Remove from heat and whisk in butter and vanilla. Cool.

Chef's tip: Use a whisk to stir. Mixture will be lumpy at first.

To prepare Caramel Sauce, combine water and sugar in a small saucepan and bring to a boil. Add this syrup to egg yolks and beat with an electric mixer for about 10 minutes. Whip cream into soft peaks and add wine. Fold into egg yolk mixture.

To serve, place apples on individual serving plates. Fill apples with Crème Pâtissière. Spoon Caramel Sauce over apples and garnish with raspberries and mint.

Chocolate Slab

with Bourbon Hazelnut Sauce

Serves 8

Tip: This recipe can easily serve 16 people.

8 egg yolks
1 cup sugar
4 cups (1 quart) heavy cream
1 cup hazelnuts, finely chopped
8 ounces semisweet chocolate, finely chopped

Sauce

3 egg yolks
½ cup sugar
1½ cups (1½ pints) heavy cream
⅓ cup hazelnuts, finely chopped
2 tablespoons bourbon

In a large, heavy-bottomed saucepan beat the egg yolks until foamy. Add sugar and beat until the mixture forms a ribbon. Pour in heavy cream and mix thoroughly. Cook over very low heat until thickened enough to coat the back of a spoon. Add hazelnuts, remove from heat, and add chocolate. Whisk until all chocolate is melted.

Line terrine dish or loaf pan with plastic wrap. Fill with chocolate mixture and cover with more plastic wrap. Place in freezer for 4 hours before serving.

Chef's tip: The sauce will keep for two or three weeks in the refrigerator.

To prepare the sauce, cook egg yolks and sugar in a large, heavy-bottomed saucepan, beating until the mixture forms a ribbon. Add cream and cook over very low heat until slightly thickened. Add hazelnuts and continue to cook until thick. Add bourbon and remove from heat. Allow to cool.

Chef's tip: The "slab" is very rich, but it will keep well in the freezer. To serve, just let it defrost slightly. A knife dipped in hot water will facilitate slicing.

To serve, ladle a spoonful of sauce onto a plate and place a slice of "slab" on the sauce.

The Cedars at Beaufort
305 Front Street
Beaufort, North Carolina
28516
919-728-7036

Innkeepers:
Bill and Pat Kwaak

Fearrington House Restaurant and Country Inn

What began as a working farm in the heart of North Carolina in the late 1700s by Jesse Fearrington's great-great-grandfather is now the setting for the internationally acclaimed Fearrington House Restaurant and Country Inn, thanks to owners R. B. and Jenny Fitch.

This creative and enthusiastic couple, native North Carolinians, purchased the 600 acres from Jesse Fearrington in 1974. Fearrington House is one of only two establishments in the United States that was honored in 1988 by the prestigious Relais & Chateaux. The members of the association practice the five C's of Relais & Chateaux hospitality: Character, Courtesy, Calm, Comfort, and Cuisine. The Fitches offer a Southern version of all five that is hard to beat anywhere.

The Fearrington House Restaurant, situated in the original home place, was opened in 1980. Wanting to retain as much charm as possible, the Fitches made few changes.

In what was once the parlor, guests gather before they are seated in one of the eight intimate dining rooms. Jenny Fitch, executive chef for many years, still directs the kitchens and works with her innovative chefs in planning the menus. Dining here is truly an exceptional experience.

This restaurant is surpassed only by the country inn the Fitches built in 1986. Inspired by their many travels to the British and French countrysides, the Fitches have borrowed the best of several worlds to create an inn that seems to have been built over a long period of time. Connecting structures surround a brick courtyard with slate walkways; there are many windows that afford a view, especially of the broad vista behind the inn. Jenny Fitch's love of fabric and art is seen at every turn. Multitalented, Jenny is responsible for selecting the colors, fabrics, paintings (many by North Carolina artists), and furnishings for the inn. The fourteen rooms have interesting roof lines, gables, alcoves, nooks, and crannies. One room, with its cozy window seat tucked under the boughs of an apple tree, has a view of the fish pool and some of the many thatched-roof birdhouses that dot the grounds.

Furnished with stripped pine antiques from England, the rooms are all different, but the amenities are the same. Quality stereo systems with a selection of tapes are provided for listening pleasure. Even the bathrooms, with cultured North Carolina marble fixtures and heated towel racks, have stereo speakers. Current magazines—including copies of *Gourmet,* which has featured Fearrington House Restaurant—and the latest novels are at bedside.

Everywhere you see Jenny's touches—the old-fashioned rose garden, the grapevine wreaths, the herb garden, and the magnificent arrangements in the Garden Room and the Tea Room, a common room where tea is served by Richard Delaney, the British innkeeper. Each afternoon at tea the guests enjoy the view of the magnificent Bynum Ridge.

A planner, builder, and merchant, R. B. Fitch has transformed this historic farm into the charming country village of Fearrington, conveniently located halfway between Chapel Hill and Pittsboro. Old farm buildings have become interesting shops, but the old silo and barn still dominate the landscape.

R. B., with his hearty laugh and great sense of humor, is responsible for the rare Belted Galloway cows that graze in the green meadow fronting the inn. The "Belties"—all with names—have become pets. In fact, they have become the official symbol of this village.

Visiting with the Fitches in the Garden Room, we thought about our love of English inns and realized we had made a wonderful discovery. As outstanding as England and France can be, everything we want in a country inn and gourmet restaurant is found in this village in the rolling hills of the North Carolina piedmont.

Miniature Glazed Orange Muffins

Yields 3 dozen miniature muffins

1 egg
¾ cup buttermilk
rind of 1 orange, grated
¼ cup orange juice
½ cup (1 stick) butter, melted
1¾ cups unbleached flour
⅓ cup sugar
1 teaspoon baking powder
½ teaspoon salt
½ teaspoon baking soda

Orange Glaze

¾ cup sugar
¾ cup orange juice
1 teaspoon lemon juice
rind of 1 orange, grated

Preheat oven to 400 degrees.

Beat egg lightly. Stir in buttermilk, orange rind, orange juice, and melted butter. Sift dry ingredients together, add to the liquid ingredients, and stir until just mixed.

Fill greased muffin cups (or use paper muffin liners) two-thirds full. Bake 20 to 25 minutes or until done.

Prepare glaze while muffins are baking. Combine all ingredients in a saucepan and stir until the sugar is dissolved. Bring mixture to a soft simmer and cook until a light syrup forms.

Remove muffins from oven. Run knife around edges of muffin cups. While the muffins are still warm, prick the tops lightly and pour glaze over. Remove from pan when cool.

Chef's tip: The batter should be lumpy; do not over mix.

Carrot Soup
with Bacon and Orange Peel

Serves 6 to 8

2 tablespoons butter
3 leeks, rinsed, cleaned, drained, and chopped
6 cups chicken stock
2 cups water
1 turnip, peeled and diced
1 potato, peeled and diced
10 carrots, peeled and diced
½ teaspoon salt
freshly ground pepper to taste
1 pint (2 cups) heavy cream

Garnish

½ cup sour cream
4 ounces bacon, fried, drained, and chopped
rind of 2 oranges, cut into ¼-inch strips and poached

Chef's tip: To add color to the soup, replace bacon with thinly sliced scallions.

Chef's tip: To add the lightest touch of sweetness to the orange rind, poach in 2 cups water and ½ cup sugar for 3 minutes.

Melt the butter and cook the leeks over medium heat for 8 to 10 minutes or until they are translucent but not browned.

Add the chicken stock, water, turnip, potato, carrots, salt, and pepper and bring to a boil. Simmer about 20 minutes or until the potato and turnip are tender. Cool slightly.

Puree in a blender or food processor. Blend in heavy cream. Heat through and serve in bowls with a dollop of sour cream and 1 tablespoon of the garnish mixture.

Small-Fry Crab Cakes
with Tarragon-Chive Mayonnaise

Yields 12 portions

8 ounces lump crabmeat, picked over to remove cartilage
¼ cup celery, finely chopped
¼ cup green or red pepper, finely chopped
4 scallions, minced
1 teaspoon lemon juice
¼ teaspoon salt
freshly ground white pepper to taste
1½ tablespoons mayonnaise
1½ tablespoons butter, melted
1¼ cups bread crumbs
2 tablespoons egg, beaten
1 teaspoon Dijon mustard
½ teaspoon Worcestershire sauce
1 tablespoon chives, chopped
4 tablespoons (½ stick) butter for sautéing

Mayonnaise

1 egg
½ teaspoon Dijon mustard
¼ teaspoon salt
1 tablespoon fresh chives, minced
1 tablespoon fresh tarragon, minced
½ lemon rind, grated
½ small clove garlic, minced
2 tablespoons lemon juice
½ cup vegetable oil
½ cup olive oil

Combine crabmeat and all ingredients except butter for sautéing. Squeeze mixture by the handful to remove excess moisture, then shape into cakes 1½ × 2½ × ½ inches thick. Sauté in butter until lightly browned.

To prepare mayonnaise, place the egg in a blender and process for 2 minutes or until mixture is thick and sticky. Add mustard, salt, herbs, lemon rind, garlic, and lemon juice. Blend thoroughly.

Combine the two oils. With the blender still running, use a baster to add the oil drop by drop until over half the oil has been added and the mixture thickens. Add the rest of the oil in a steady stream until mixture is creamy.

Serve crab cakes with mayonnaise.

Chef's tip: If the mayonnaise refuses to thicken or has curdled, blend together 1 teaspoon prepared mustard and 1 tablespoon of the mayonnaise in a clean bowl. Beat for a few seconds until the sauce has thickened or smoothed. Add the rest of the turned sauce by the teaspoonful, beating after each addition.

Pecan Chicken
with Leeks, Country Ham, and Honey Mustard Butter

Serves 6

Honey Mustard Butter

1 cup bourbon
3 tablespoons shallots, chopped
4 ounces (½ cup) honey
1 tablespoon Dijon mustard
3 tablespoons coarse mustard
½ pound (2 sticks) butter, softened
salt and pepper to taste

Tip: Do not let butter soften too much, or it is difficult to shape into a log. Roll in waxed paper and refrigerate until ready to use.

Pecan Chicken

1 cup pecans, chopped
½ cup fresh bread crumbs, toasted
2 eggs, beaten
1 tablespoon water
6 6- to 7-ounce boneless chicken breasts
¼ cup whole wheat flour
2 medium leeks
4 ounces country ham
4 tablespoons (½ stick) butter
freshly ground pepper
½ cup clarified butter

Tip: To clarify butter, place butter in a saucepan over moderate heat until melted. Reduce heat and skim off any foam. Cook on low heat until milky solids collect on the bottom of pan and liquid is clear. Strain out residue.

To prepare Honey Mustard Butter, place bourbon and shallots in a small saucepan and cook over low heat until the mixture is reduced by half. Cool. Combine with remaining ingredients, shape into a log, and refrigerate.

To prepare Pecan Chicken, combine the pecans and bread crumbs in a shallow pan and set aside. In a separate deep bowl, beat eggs with water and set aside.

Bread the chicken by lightly flouring it, dipping in egg wash, and coating with pecan mixture. Refrigerate for 15 to 30 minutes.

Trim leeks and rinse under running water. Julienne leeks and country ham and sauté in butter in medium skillet until the leeks are translucent but not browned. Season with pepper and set aside.

Sauté chicken in clarified butter, cooking evenly on both sides.

To serve, place the chicken breasts on a bed of leeks and country ham. Top with a pat of Honey Mustard Butter.

Veal Loin Roast

Serves 6 to 8

1 tablespoon butter
1 tablespoon olive oil
3½ to 4 pounds veal loin (center cut)
½ cup chicken stock
½ teaspoon salt
freshly ground white pepper
1 bouquet garni (thyme, oregano, bay leaf, and parsley)
⅓ cup white wine
2 tablespoons flour
salt and white pepper to taste
1 cup (½ pint) heavy cream
fresh parsley, minced, for garnish

Chef's tip: This roast makes an elegant though expensive meal. Allow ½ pound of veal per person and then a little extra just to be certain. The roast may be stuffed with sprigs of fresh thyme and marjoram if you have the butcher put the herbs inside before it is tied.

Preheat oven to 325 degrees.

Melt the butter in a heavy roasting pan and add olive oil. Brown the veal thoroughly. Add chicken stock, salt, pepper, and bouquet garni. Cover and roast about 2 hours, basting often. Remove from oven when meat thermometer reads 175 degrees (25 to 30 minutes per pound).

Remove veal from pan and deglaze pan with white wine. Remove and set aside all but 2 tablespoons of stock from the pan. Add flour to the stock in the pan and cook, stirring constantly for 2 minutes. Strain the set-aside juices and slowly add back to flour and stock mixture, whisking slowly until thickened. Add salt, pepper, and heavy cream. Heat through.

Slice the roast and arrange slices in an overlapping fashion on the serving plate. Cover lightly with the sauce and garnish with minced parsley.

Roast Leg of Lamb
with Braised Scallion Sauce

Serves 6

1 leg of lamb (about 8 pounds), boned
rind of 4 lemons, chopped
10 garlic cloves, chopped
4 lemons, juiced
1 teaspoon salt
3 teaspoons pepper, freshly ground
½ bunch parsley, chopped
2 teaspoons fresh rosemary, chopped
1 teaspoon fresh thyme, chopped
½ cup olive oil

Chef's tip: The roast should be removed from the oven when the internal temperature reaches 165 degrees. It will continue to cook for a few minutes and the temperature will continue to rise.

Sauce

18 scallions
1 tablespoon butter
1½ cups chicken stock
3 tablespoons sugar
¼ teaspoon salt
¼ teaspoon white pepper, freshly ground
⅓ cup heavy cream
2 tablespoons Dijon mustard

Mix the lemon rind, lemon juice, garlic, salt, pepper, herbs, and oil. Marinate the lamb in this mixture for 24 hours.

Preheat oven to 375 degrees.

Roll and tie the marinated lamb. Coat outside with the remaining marinade. Roast uncovered, fat side up, on a rack until meat thermometer reads 165 degrees (approximately 20 minutes per pound).

Chef's tip: A variation of this sauce can be made using leeks braised in the same butter, chicken stock, and sugar. It is a delightful accompaniment to steaks or other red meats. Serve with a sprinkle of freshly grated Parmesan cheese.

To prepare the sauce, wash and clean the scallions and trim the tops off, leaving about 1 inch of green.

Melt butter in a heavy skillet and add chicken stock and sugar. Bring to a boil and add scallions, salt, and pepper. Cook partially covered over medium-low heat until scallions can be pierced with a fork. Remove from pan and set aside.

Raise heat in skillet to slightly reduce liquid. Add heavy cream and mustard. Simmer and stir until sauce is smooth and slightly reduced. Add scallions to the pan to warm.

To serve, slice the lamb and top with sauce and 2 or 3 scallions.

Sautéed Button Mushrooms
with Brandy

Serves 8

1½ pounds fresh mushrooms
2 tablespoons butter
2 cloves garlic, minced
1 tablespoon lemon juice
1½ tablespoons brandy
½ cup heavy cream
Parmesan cheese, grated
bread crumbs, toasted

Wipe mushrooms with a damp paper towel to clean. Remove stems and reserve for another use.

Melt butter in a large skillet and add mushroom caps and minced garlic. Drizzle with lemon juice and cook over medium-high heat, rolling the mushrooms in the pan to cook evenly. Add brandy. After 5 to 10 minutes, pour in the heavy cream and reduce slightly.

To serve, sprinkle with Parmesan cheese and toasted bread crumbs.

Chef's tip: To make bread crumbs, remove crusts from good-quality bread. Roll pieces between the palms of hands (the food processor makes too fine a crumb). Toast until golden brown and store until ready to use.

Baked Acorn Squash
with Spinach and Pine Nuts

Serves 6 to 8

3 to 4 acorn squash
(3½ inches in diameter)
4 tablespoons butter
½ teaspoon salt
freshly ground pepper
freshly grated nutmeg
3 tablespoons pine nuts
3 pounds fresh spinach

Preheat oven to 375 degrees.

Cut squash in half and remove seeds. Melt 1 tablespoon butter and brush all cut surfaces. Season with ¼ teaspoon salt, pepper, and nutmeg. Cover with foil and bake (cut side up) for 35 minutes or until tender when pierced with a fork. Remove from oven and set aside but keep warm.

Melt 1 tablespoon butter in a small skillet and sauté pine nuts until golden brown. Set aside to drain on absorbent towels.

Wash spinach to remove any grit. Remove the coarse main stem. Cook spinach in a large skillet over medium-high heat using only the water that clings to the leaves after washing. When spinach wilts, add the remaining butter and salt, pepper, nutmeg, and pine nuts. Heat through, spoon mixture into squash, and serve.

Fresh Coconut Cake
with Rum and Orange Filling

Yields one 9-inch, four-layer cake

Note: A coconut cake is a traditional holiday dessert in the South. This cake's delicious flavor comes from including grated orange rind in the batter, orange juice and rum in the layers, and an orange filling between the layers. It may be made well in advance and frozen.

¾ cup butter, softened
2 cups sugar
3 egg yolks
2 cups flour
2 teaspoons baking powder
¼ teaspoon salt
¾ cup milk
3 egg whites
rind of 1 orange, grated
¼ cup orange juice
½ cup rum

Filling

1 cup sugar
¼ teaspoon salt
4 tablespoons cornstarch
1 cup orange juice
2 tablespoons butter
rind of 1 orange, grated
2 tablespoons lemon juice

Icing

1 cup (½ pint) heavy cream
2 teaspoons rum
⅓ cup sugar
meat of 1 fresh coconut, grated

Chef's tip: To prepare the fresh coconut, drive a nail in the end of a coconut and drain the milk from it. Bake the coconut at 350 degrees for 20 to 25 minutes or until the outer shell cracks. This process makes the meat easier to remove from the shell. Cut the meat into chunks and grate it in a food processor.

Preheat oven to 350 degrees.

Grease bottoms of two 9-inch cake pans. Cut wax paper to fit bottoms, and grease and flour the wax paper. Set aside.

Cream butter and sugar until light and fluffy. Beat in egg yolks one at a time. Sift flour, baking powder, and salt together. Add butter and egg mixture alternating with milk, beginning and ending with dry ingredients. Set aside.

Whip egg whites until stiff but not dry. Fold into cake batter along with the grated orange rind.

Pour batter into pans and bake for about 25 minutes or until toothpick inserted in the middle comes out clean. Let layers cool in the pans for a few minutes, invert onto rack, and peel off wax paper.

Slice layers in half to get four thin layers. Prick each layer with a fork, and drizzle with the mixture of orange juice and rum. Set aside.

To prepare filling, blend sugar, salt, and cornstarch in a saucepan. Gradually add orange juice and bring to a boil. Boil 1 to 2 minutes, remove from heat, and stir in butter, orange rind, and lemon juice. Cool. Spread one-third of the mixture on the first layer; stack the second and third layers, spreading filling between each. Top with the last layer.

To prepare icing, whip the cream until soft peaks form and add the rum and sugar. Continue to whip until stiff. Spread over the cake and pat shredded coconut onto the sides and top and serve.

Tip: Use a cake-layer cutter to slice layers. Also be sure not to poke the fork all the way through the cake.

Fearrington House Restaurant and Country Inn
Fearrington Village Center
U.S. Highway 15/501
Pittsboro,
North Carolina 27312
919-542-4000,
800-334-5475

Innkeeper:
Richard Delaney

Glendale Springs Inn and Restaurant

The bright lights of Broadway and Hollywood are a far cry from the small village of Glendale Springs in the Blue Ridge Mountains where Gayle Winston owns the historic Glendale Springs Inn.

North Carolinian Gayle Winston first went to New York, after graduating from Bridgewater College in Virginia, as an aspiring journalist. She became an editorial researcher for *Time* magazine and befriended a struggling young playwright named Leslie Clark Stevens III, who then worked as a copyboy. Soon, their lunch hours were used for rehearsal time and Gayle found herself the producer of his highly successful off-Broadway play, *Bullfight*, at the age of twenty-three. She went on to produce four productions on Broadway and to marry Ron Winston, a leading writer and television and film director.

It was after her husband's untimely death in 1973 that Gayle returned to the mountains near Grassy Creek, North Carolina, to her great-grandfather's farm, where she intended to "rock on the porch and can pickles." Her retirement was short-lived. Soon she found herself raising cattle and planting vegetables and herbs—and, at the same time, cultivating her interest in food, which first began in New York where she was introduced to gourmet cuisine. This love of cooking led her to open the Trout Dale Dining Room, located just over the Virginia line, in 1975. For five years she ran the popular restaurant with friends.

Attending a Glendale Springs auction in 1980, Gayle could not resist buying the three-story, Queen Anne–style house she remembered from her childhood spent in that area. The house, listed in the National Register of Historic Places, was built in the 1890s by General John Adams and has an interesting history. It served as a wayside inn, spa, meeting house, dance hall, rooming house, and headquarters for the Works Progress Administration during the construction of the Blue Ridge Parkway. Gayle saw it as an inn where she could serve French-inspired food. Later she offered lodging, beginning with only one room which was generally requested by newlyweds who married at the inn and wished overnight accommodations. An additional five rooms were soon opened due to the demand. Recently six were added in a newer structure across the road.

Simple down-home furniture is used in the guest rooms, with quilts made by Gayle's mother, great-grandmother, and aunt. Another aunt made the colorful hand-hooked rugs. There are no telephones and no television—only the sounds of bluebirds chirping and the cool mountain breezes, which carry the wonderful aromas from the inn's bakery.

There is much to do in the Glendale Springs area. Plan a picnic and take along one of the inn's box lunches with a loaf of freshly baked bread. Canoe the New River, hike, bike, shop for antiques and crafts, and make sure you see the frescoes at Holy Trinity Episcopal Church. They alone are worth the trip.

Friends and visitors rave about Gayle's special touch in all three of her establishments: Glendale Springs Inn, Old Salem Tavern, and at Stars, located in Winston-Salem's Stevens Center, a theater for the performing arts. The show definitely still goes on for Gayle Winston.

Limpa Rye Bread

Yields two round loaves

Chef's tip: Liquid that is too hot will kill the yeast, so be sure to check temperature of milk.

½ cup whole wheat flour
½ cup rye flour
½ cup oatmeal
½ cup brown sugar, firmly packed
1½ teaspoons salt
2 cups milk (heated to 120 degrees)
rind of 2 oranges, grated
1 tablespoon yeast
2 tablespoons vegetable oil
5 cups all-purpose flour

Mix whole wheat and rye flours, oatmeal, sugar, and salt together in a large bowl. Heat milk and orange rind together. Dissolve yeast in milk mixture and add to dry ingredients, mixing until smooth. Cover and let rise in warm place for about 1 to 1½ hours or until double in size.

Mix oil and 4 cups of flour with sponge mixture. Turn onto a floured surface and knead in remaining flour. Place in a greased bowl and let rise for about 1 hour in a warm place. Punch down and divide in half. Roll each portion into a tight ball and place on a greased cookie sheet sprinkled with cornmeal. Let rise again for about 1 hour or until doubled.

Preheat oven to 325 degrees.

Bake for about 45 minutes to 1 hour. Cool on rack and brush with melted butter and serve.

Tip: We especially liked this Swedish bread served warm with cheese and apple cider.

Mushroom-Onion Soup Gratinée

Serves 6 to 8

½ cup Herbed Butter
2 large onions, thinly sliced
½ cup dry white wine
2 cups chicken broth, preferably homemade
2 cups beef broth
1 bay leaf
¼ teaspoon dried thyme leaves
1 teaspoon Beurre Manié
3 tablespoons dry sherry
2 tablespoons butter
2½ cups mushrooms, thinly sliced
French bread, toasted (1 slice per serving, crust removed)
1½ to 2 cups Gruyère cheese, grated (¼ cup per serving)

Herbed Butter

½ cup (1 stick) unsalted butter, softened
1 clove garlic, minced
2 teaspoons chives, minced
2 teaspoons parsley, minced

Beurre Manié

2 tablespoons Herbed Butter
2 tablespoons flour

Prepare Herbed Butter by combining all ingredients and blending thoroughly. Reserve 2 tablespoons for Beurre Manié.

Sauté onions very slowly in the remaining Herbed Butter until soft but not brown. Add dry white wine, chicken and beef broths, bay leaf, and thyme. Simmer 15 minutes.

While soup mixture is simmering, prepare the Beurre Manié. Combine 2 tablespoons Herbed Butter with flour, working together with tips of fingers or a spoon.

Stir Beurre Manié into soup, add dry sherry, and set aside.

Very lightly sauté mushrooms in butter and add to soup.

Preheat broiler.

Ladle soup into ovenproof cups, top with toasted French bread and grated cheese. Run cups under broiler to reheat soup and to melt cheese. Serve immediately.

Chef's tip: Keeping Herbed Butter in the refrigerator at all times is one of those tricks that produces results just short of magic. For almost-instant garlic bread, for instance, spread Herbed Butter on thick-cut slices of French bread and toast. Use any choice of herbs.

Chef's tip: Both the Herbed Butter and Beurre Manié can be made in large batches, formed into a cylinder, and wrapped tightly in plastic wrap or waxed paper. Refrigerate (or freeze), then slice and use as needed. (Be sure to label them—they look alike.)

Chef's tip: Beurre Manié is also a good thickener for gravy.

Herbed Crepes
with Gruyère Filling

Yields twelve 7-inch or about forty 3-inch crepes

Chef's tip: These crepes are seasoned to be appetizers. For dessert crepes, omit the herbs and add a bit of sugar. For main-dish crepes, vary the seasonings to complement the filling.

1 cup flour
1½ teaspoons salt
3 eggs
3 egg yolks
12-ounce can beer
1½ tablespoons sour cream
6 tablespoons (¾ stick) butter, melted
1 tablespoon chives, finely chopped
½ tablespoon tarragon, finely chopped
1 tablespoon parsley, finely chopped
butter for greasing crepe pan

Filling

4 tablespoons (½ stick) butter
½ large onion, minced
¾ cup flour
1½ cups milk
1 teaspoon salt
nutmeg to taste, freshly ground
white pepper to taste
½ pound Gruyère cheese, cubed

Assembly Ingredients

3 eggs, beaten
3 tablespoons flour
fresh bread crumbs
oil for deep-frying (optional)

In a blender or food processor, combine flour, salt, eggs, egg yolks, beer, and sour cream. Blend well, then stir in melted butter. Add herbs and stir.

Melt about ¼ teaspoon butter in a 7-inch crepe pan or nonstick skillet. Pour 2 or 3 tablespoons of batter into the pan, tilting the pan in all directions until the batter coats the bottom of the pan. When edges of crepe begin to brown, flip it over with a spatula and lightly brown the second side. Repeat the process, using remaining batter. Set crepes aside.

To prepare filling, sauté onion in butter until translucent. Add flour and mix well. Add milk, salt, nutmeg, and white pepper. Cook until bubbling and thickened. Remove from heat, let cool to lukewarm, then add cheese, stirring until blended.

To assemble crepes, mix eggs with flour. Place about 3 tablespoons full of cheese filling on each crepe. Fold over like a turnover and seal with egg and flour mixture. Brush egg and flour mixture on the outside of crepe and coat with fresh bread crumbs. Deep-fry at 375 degrees until golden, or bake in oven at 375 degrees until golden. Serve immediately.

Chef's tip: The usual "resting" period for crepes is not necessary with this recipe.

Chef's tip: The generous amount of butter in the batter makes it unnecessary to grease a seasoned crepe pan for each crepe. The pan, of course, should be used only for crepes or omelets. Keep batter well mixed while making the crepes.

Chef's tip: Add more milk if filling is too thick. It should be much thicker than a traditional Béchamel.

Chef's tip: Crepes can be assembled a day ahead and then deep-fried or baked before serving.

Shrimp with Shiitake Mushrooms
and Garlic Basil Butter

Serves 4

½ cup (1 stick) butter, softened
3 cloves garlic, chopped
2 tablespoons fresh basil, chopped
salt and pepper to taste
2 tablespoons olive oil
½ pound shrimp, peeled and deveined
½ cup shiitake mushroom caps
angel hair pasta (optional)

Tip: If shiitake mushrooms are unavailable, use regular fresh mushrooms.

To make Garlic Basil Butter, combine butter, garlic, basil, salt, and pepper. Mix until evenly blended and set aside.

Heat olive oil in a sauté pan. Add the shrimp and mushrooms and cook for 2 to 3 minutes. Add 2 or 3 tablespoons of the butter mixture and continue cooking until shrimp are done.

Serve with angel hair pasta if desired.

Tip: Garlic Basil Butter is great with any pasta.

Chef's tip: Do not overcook shrimp. They should be cooked just long enough to have color and firmness.

Beef with Shallots
and Red Wine Vinegar

Serves 1

6-ounce beef filet
2 tablespoons butter
1 tablespoon vegetable oil
1 shallot, finely diced
¼ cup red wine vinegar
¼ cup heavy cream
lemon juice, salt, and pepper to taste
chopped herbs (parsley, basil, chervil, or tarragon) for garnish

In a small skillet melt 1 tablespoon butter and 1 tablespoon oil on high heat. Sear both sides of filet, cook to the desired doneness, and set aside (for medium-rare filet, cook to 120 degrees on meat thermometer).

Add remaining butter and shallot to the skillet and cook until shallot is wilted or golden. Add wine vinegar and whisk. Add heavy cream and whisk again. Bring to a rapid boil and reduce liquid by half. Add lemon juice, salt, and pepper to taste.

Spoon sauce onto a warm plate and place cooked steak on top. Sprinkle with chopped herbs.

Chef's tip: For a slight variation, add softened butter to the shallot and vinegar mixture instead of cream, whisking constantly. Do not heat. Butter should not be melted and oily.

Veal Marengo

Serves 6

2 pounds boned veal loin, cubed (1-inch to 1½-inch pieces)
flour
½ cup olive oil
1 cup onion, coarsely chopped
salt and pepper to taste
4 teaspoons flour
1 cup dry white wine
1 cup veal stock
3 cups ripe tomatoes, blanched, peeled, seeded, and chopped
4 cloves garlic, crushed
1 bay leaf
pinch of thyme
2 tablespoons butter
12 small button mushrooms
6 puffed pastry shells

Chef's tip: Puff pastry shells are found in the frozen food section of your grocery store. Allow the veal to spill down the sides of shells for a nice effect.

Lightly dust veal with flour. Heat olive oil in a large pan and brown veal cubes on all sides. Add ½ cup chopped onion, salt, pepper, and flour. Stir until the mixture is smooth and blended. Continue stirring and add white wine and veal stock. Bring to boil. Add tomatoes, garlic, bay leaf, and thyme. Cover the pan, lower heat, and simmer about 45 minutes or until veal is tender.

Chef's tip: When you add the onion and mushrooms, you can also add about 1 cup of black olives for an interesting taste.

In separate pan, melt butter and sauté remaining ½ cup onion and mushrooms until onions are translucent. Add onion and mushrooms to veal mixture and cook for about 15 minutes longer. Remove pan from heat and skim off any fat that rises to the top. Reheat veal and serve on puffed pastry shells.

Grapefruit Ice Cream Glendale

Serves 4 to 6

1 cup grapefruit juice
¼ to ½ cup sugar, depending on sweetness of fruit
1 cup (½ pint) heavy cream
1 tablespoon lemon juice
pinch of salt

Mix all ingredients and chill. Freeze in ice cream maker according to manufacturer's directions. Serve.

Note: Glendale Springs Inn also makes ice cream from old-fashioned huckleberries, gooseberries, mulberries, wild blackberries, raspberries, and wineberries. All of these are very seedy and must be pureed and strained, but they make incredibly flavorful desserts. The basic recipe is:
1 part berry puree, uncooked
½ part sugar
1 part heavy cream
squeeze of lemon juice

Tip: For ice cream that is pretty as well as good, use pink grapefruit and do not strain the pulp.

Orange Flan
with Chocolate Grand Marnier Sauce

Serves 12

rind of 2 oranges, grated
4 cups milk
8 eggs
1 cup sugar
1 tablespoon Triple Sec
mint sprigs, orange sections (optional)

Sauce

½ pound semisweet chocolate chips
½ cup water, boiled
2 tablespoons butter, softened
1 tablespoon Grand Marnier

Preheat oven to 325 degrees.

Scald milk with orange rind. Beat eggs and sugar together. Add milk mixture to egg mixture. Add Triple Sec. Strain rind from mixture. Divide into twelve 6-ounce custard cups. Place in a roasting pan with water filled halfway up the custard cups. Bake for 20 to 30 minutes or until small knife inserted in center comes out clean. Cool on rack and refrigerate.

To prepare sauce, pour boiling water over chocolate chips. Whisk until smooth, then whisk in butter and Grand Marnier.

Unmold custard cups and serve warm sauce over flan.

Tip: This is a delightful dessert with or without the sauce.

Chef's tip: To serve, place two orange sections and a sprig of mint on top of each custard. Pour sauce on rim of plate between two additional orange sections.

Glendale Springs Inn
and Restaurant
Glendale Springs,
North Carolina 28629
919-982-2102

Innkeeper:
Gayle Winston

Gideon Ridge Inn

The view from the stone terrace of Gideon Ridge Inn was even more dramatic than we expected. This rambling, two-story inn, built of stone carved from Grandfather Mountain, conforms with the ridge overlooking some of the oldest mountains in the world.

After a warm welcome from Cobb and Jane Milner, the innkeepers, we made our way to the terrace, where the summits were rising out of white mist, making it appear to be an ocean with mountains coming up from the floor. As the clouds lifted, the Blue Ridge Mountains turned an even darker blue; the first leaves of fall glowed in the sunlight.

To discover an inn with such a spectacular view and then find each guest room and the carriage house suite so tastefully decorated was a delightful surprise. Our favorite room, warmed by a fire from the white marble fireplace, had a massive, hand-carved Edwardian bed. The fresh flowers and current magazines were extra amenities.

The Milners came from New Jersey to look for a home in Jane's native state. Instead, they found an inn, which had been originally built as a summer home for the nephew of one of Blowing Rock's most noted benefactors, Moses Cone. The Milners, realizing the house was too large for a private residence and yet knowing they could not walk away from it, became innkeepers overnight.

Jane, the competent chef, learned about foods from her family's cooks as she grew up in North Carolina. In turn, she taught her daughter, Susan Milner McCall, who has also worked in the finest restaurants in Washington, D.C. It was Susan's professional know-how and experience that helped her parents open their dining room to inn guests and to the public by prior arrangement.

This charming, secluded inn is reached by a narrow street off the main road to Blowing Rock, one of the most famous tourist attractions in North Carolina. Ask the Milners to tell you more about the ancient Indian legend concerning this phenomenon, which has attracted visitors since as early as 1845. See the rock, explore to your heart's content, and then return to Gideon Ridge and warm yourself from the cool, crisp mountain air before a crackling fire in the gigantic stone fireplace. What better way to end a day in the high country.

Whether it's honeymooners desiring a romantic getaway, bridge players only wanting to be interrupted for fresh, delicious meals, or corporate executives retreating to unwind, Gideon Ridge Inn is the place to be.

Cornmeal Pancakes

Serves 10 to 12

2 cups white cornmeal
2 tablespoons sugar
2 teaspoons salt
2 cups boiling water
2 eggs
1 cup milk
4 tablespoons butter, melted
1 cup unbleached flour, sifted
4 teaspoons baking powder
fresh raspberries for garnish (optional)

Combine cornmeal, sugar, and salt in large bowl. Add boiling water and stir until mixture is free of lumps. Cover and allow to rest for at least 15 minutes.

Beat eggs slightly, add milk, and set aside. Melt butter and set aside to cool.

Sift together flour and baking powder and set aside.

Add egg and milk mixture and butter to cornmeal mixture. Beat until smooth. Stir in sifted flour but do not overmix. Batter should be slightly lumpy.

Cook on hot griddle that has been greased. Brown on both sides, garnish with fresh raspberries, and serve with butter and warm maple syrup.

Chef's tip: Pancakes should be browned sufficiently on the first side because they should be turned only once.

Summer Squash Soup

Serves 8 to 10

2 tablespoons butter
8 scallions, chopped
6 medium yellow squash, chopped
3 cups chicken stock
2 cups (1 pint) heavy cream
nutmeg, salt, and pepper to taste
parsley, minced, for garnish

Heat butter in saucepan and sauté scallions until golden. Add squash and chicken stock. Cook for about 15 minutes or until squash is tender. Allow to cool slightly and puree in a food processor or blender until smooth. Season to taste with nutmeg, salt, and pepper. Add cream and reheat carefully over low fire to serve hot, or chill and serve cold. Garnish with parsley.

Chef's tip: Puree squash mixture in batches.

Susan's Chicken

Serves 4 to 6

Chef's tip: This recipe is easily expanded for more people.

Chef's tip: Drop the tomatoes in boiling water for about 1 minute, then peel; or use a 16-ounce can of tomatoes and juice.

Chef's tip: Use the bottom of an iron skillet to pound chicken if a mallet is not available.

4 tablespoons olive oil
1 green pepper, seeded and chopped
1 large Spanish onion, peeled and chopped
2 cloves garlic, minced
4 large ripe tomatoes, peeled, seeded, and chopped
6 to 12 large ripe olives, pitted and quartered
½ teaspoon oregano
½ teaspoon thyme
2 bay leaves
2 tablespoons fresh parsley, minced (or 1 tablespoon if dried)
cayenne pepper, freshly ground black pepper, and salt to taste
4 chicken breasts, boned
½ cup dry white wine (use more if needed)
Perfect Rice

Heat 2 tablespoons olive oil in a large sauté pan. Sauté green pepper, onion, and garlic. Add tomatoes, olives, herbs, and seasonings. Cover and cook for 25 minutes.

Pound the chicken breasts to ¼-inch thickness. Heat 2 tablespoons of olive oil in skillet and sauté chicken for 8 to 10 minutes. Keep warm on a platter.

Deglaze the pan with the wine. Add tomato mixture to the wine. Heat and spoon over the chicken breasts. Serve with Perfect Rice.

Perfect Rice

Serves 8 to 12

2 cups regular long-grain rice
1 tablespoon salt
½ cup (1 stick) butter
6 to 8 scallions, chopped and sautéed (optional)
1 small onion or several shallots, minced (optional)

Preheat oven to 300 degrees.

In an 8-quart pot, bring a large quantity of water to a boil. Add salt. Slowly add rice. Stir once, then boil rapidly for 12 minutes. Drain the rice in a colander and rinse briefly under cold water.

Chef's tip: Rice can be held warm for an hour or so until served.

Melt butter in a 4-quart casserole dish. Add scallions and onion. Spoon drained rice into dish, cover, and set in a warm oven 10 to 15 minutes. Serve.

Feta Cheese Timbales
with Creamed Spinach

Serves 8

16 ounces feta cheese
6 eggs
2 cups (1 pint) heavy cream
white pepper, freshly ground

Creamed Spinach

2 10-ounce packages fresh or frozen spinach
¼ cup onion, minced
4 tablespoons butter
2 tablespoons flour
2 cups (1 pint) heavy cream
nutmeg and white pepper to taste

Preheat oven to 350 degrees.

Butter eight 4-ounce timbale molds or ramekins. In a food processor or blender, process cheese, eggs, cream, and pepper together for 3 or 4 minutes. Divide mixture equally into molds. Place molds on a rack in a pan of hot (not boiling) water. Water level should be even with the mixture inside the molds. Cover loosely with foil. Bake for 45 minutes or until knife blade inserted in middle comes out clean. The timbales should be puffed up and firm. If not, return to oven for 5 minutes and test again for doneness.

Chef's tip: If timbale is still not done, continue cooking for 5 minutes or until done.

Carefully remove molds from pan and cool for 5 minutes. Gently run a knife around edges and invert each timbale onto a plate.

Prepare Creamed Spinach while timbales are baking. If using fresh spinach, wash and cook for 3 minutes in boiling water and drain. Rinse with cold water and drain. If using frozen spinach, thaw and drain well.

Chef's tip: Creamed Spinach may be prepared ahead and kept warm in a hot water bath. Cover with wax paper and a tightly fitting lid.

Chop spinach well and set aside. Melt 1 tablespoon butter and sauté onion. Add to spinach. Set aside.

In a saucepan melt 3 tablespoons butter and stir in flour. Cook for 2 to 3 minutes without browning. Add heavy cream, using whisk to stir until thickened. Stir in spinach and onion mixture. Season with nutmeg, white pepper, and salt to taste and heat over low flame.

Arrange spinach around timbale and serve.

Filet of Beef Gideon Ridge

Serves 12

1 whole filet of beef

Marinade

1 lemon, thinly sliced
2 carrots, thinly sliced
1 onion, thinly sliced
3 sprigs parsley, chopped
½ teaspoon dried thyme
1 bay leaf
freshly ground white pepper
½ cup olive or corn oil
2 slices bacon
½ cup Madeira wine for deglazing pan
watercress for garnish

Trim a whole filet. Remove excess fat and sinew. Tie at 2-inch intervals to hold shape.

Combine all marinade ingredients and allow beef to marinate for several hours, turning often and allowing filet to come to room temperature.

Preheat oven to 500 degrees.

Remove filet from marinade and place on broiler rack. Place bacon on top of filet. Place in middle of oven and turn heat down to 350 degrees. Roast for 35 minutes. Remove from pan. Place on platter, cover loosely with foil, and keep in warm oven for up to 30 minutes.

Deglaze broiler pan with wine. Slice filet into 1-inch thick slices, spoon deglazing liquid over the slices, garnish with watercress, and serve.

Chef's tip: Filet of beef is usually served rare—120 degrees on a meat thermometer.

Casserole of Summer Vegetables

Serves 8 to 10

4 medium potatoes
4 zucchini
6 medium tomatoes
3 garlic cloves, peeled
⅓ cup olive oil
1 tablespoon fresh or dried basil, chopped
salt and pepper to taste

Preheat oven to 400 degrees.

Slice unpeeled vegetables into ¼-inch slices. Alternate vegetables and arrange in overlapping rows in a 10- × 15-inch baking dish. Spear garlic on toothpicks and place among vegetables. Drizzle with olive oil, then sprinkle with basil, salt, and pepper. Bake uncovered 30 to 40 minutes, remove garlic, and serve.

Gideon Ridge Inn
6148 Gideon Ridge Road
P.O. Box 1929
Blowing Rock,
North Carolina 28605
704-295-3644

Innkeepers: Cobb and Jane Milner

Ragged Garden Inn and Restaurant

Joe Villani is the personable chef-owner of Ragged Garden Inn. As we chatted over coffee in the main dining room, Joe traced his roots to Parma, where his parents were born. We enjoyed the roaring fire in the massive fireplace while Joe shared stories of his Italian family and heritage. The dedicated son of immigrants, he credits his mother as being "the best cook in the family" and the inspiration for his love of Italian cooking.

His first introduction to a commercial kitchen was as a trainee at the world-famous Sardi's Restaurant in New York City. He later owned several large restaurants in Connecticut and Florida. He and his charming wife, Joyce, had always dreamed of owning a small inn where he could serve classic Italian cuisine to guests. Ragged Garden Inn is a dream come true.

It was around the turn of the century that Blowing Rock, a small village in the Blue Ridge Mountains on the Eastern Continental Divide, began to thrive. Inns, hotels, boardinghouses, and summer homes were built as an escape from the heat of the lowlands. The 4,000-foot elevation meant cool days and chilly nights. Built as a summer home in 1900, Ragged Garden is situated on an acre of land, surrounded by a garden of roses, rhododendrons, dogwoods, and apple trees. The handsome structure is built of native stone and siding made from chestnut bark slabs.

Following their purchase of the house in 1982, the Villanis restored Ragged Garden from top to bottom. The large, comfortable guest rooms are reached by a unique staircase of native stone and slate. From the upstairs windows you can see Main Street of Blowing Rock, only a block away, where shops, art galleries, parks, and local attractions are found. It's a shopper's paradise offering everything from country crafts to priceless antiques.

Ragged Garden's main dining room, with antique chandeliers, offers a warm and inviting place for diners. There are additional dining areas, private and formal, which are very attractive settings for special dinner parties and wedding receptions.

The morning of our departure, we visited the kitchen and were greeted with aromas only to be found in an Italian chef's domain. Our sole disappointment was not being able to savor the minestrone simmering on the stove. But we did not depart empty-handed, as Joe offered us some of his tasty cornichon sauce.

As we left Ragged Garden Inn, we were especially impressed with the new chapters the Villanis have written in the history of this popular mountain inn.

Minestrone

Serves 10 to 12

Chef's tip: If using canned broth, be careful it is not too salty.

Tip: Wash and soak dried beans in water for several hours prior to cooking to ensure their tenderness. Do not add salt.

Chef's tip: Be sure to use only a handful of pasta. If soup gets too thick, add more broth or water.

¼ cup olive oil
¼ cup (½ stick) butter
1 large onion, coarsely chopped
bunch of fresh parsley, minced
4 or 5 cloves garlic, minced
3 cups chicken broth
2 cups water
¾ cup dried northern or pinto beans
1 cup fresh green beans
3 stalks celery, diced
3 carrots, diced
⅓ head cabbage, chopped
2 medium zucchini, diced
2 teaspoons tomato paste
1 cup of pasta (very small elbows if possible)
salt and pepper to taste
pinch of nutmeg, freshly grated
6 to 7 basil leaves, minced, or ½ teaspoon dry
freshly grated Parmesan cheese for garnish

In a large pot melt butter and oil together over medium-low heat. Add onion and parsley, and cook for 5 minutes. Add garlic and simmer until onion is translucent. Add broth, water, dry beans, and tomato paste. Boil gently for 20 minutes. Add green beans, celery, and carrots, and cook for 10 minutes. Add cabbage and cook for 10 minutes. Add zucchini and cook for 30 minutes. Add pasta, salt, pepper, nutmeg, and basil. Continue cooking for 1½ hours. Garnish with freshly grated Parmesan cheese and serve.

Swiss Cheese Dressing

Yields 1 gallon

Chef's tip: This dressing keeps well for at least three months in the refrigerator. It is also a fine dip.

Chef's tip: Add chives, curry, or garlic if desired.

Tip: This recipe can easily be reduced by half. Just be careful about the amount of onion used.

1 pound Swiss cheese, grated fine
1 gallon mayonnaise
1 medium onion, grated fine
¼ cup Dijon mustard
¼ cup red wine vinegar
dash of Worcestershire sauce
salt and pepper to taste

Blend all ingredients together well, pour into large containers, and store in refrigerator until ready to use.

Saltimbocca alla Romana

Serves 4

8 slices veal, thinly sliced and pounded
salt and pepper to taste
½ cup all-purpose flour
2 tablespoons butter
8 thin slices prosciutto ham
8 thin slices mozzarella cheese

Preheat broiler.

Sprinkle salt and pepper on each slice of veal. Dredge veal in flour; pat and remove any excess flour. Melt butter in sauté pan over high heat. When butter foams, place veal in pan. Do not crowd. Sauté 1 minute each side. Place veal in ovenproof serving dish. Top with prosciutto and cheese. Place dish 4 inches under broiler just until cheese melts. Serve immediately.

Chef's tip: Serve with buttered spinach linguine.

Risotto alla Pana

Serves 4

3 tablespoons butter
1 medium onion, finely chopped
1 cup uncooked rice, washed
4 to 5 cups chicken stock, warmed
½ cup heavy cream
4 to 5 teaspoons Parmesan cheese, grated

Melt butter in a heavy pot over low heat. Add onion and cook until soft and translucent. Add rice and mix until rice is well coated with butter mixture, then add 1 cup stock and cook until rice absorbs all the liquid. Continue adding stock 1 cup at a time until rice is cooked. Stir in cream and cheese and serve in soup bowls.

Tip: Allow at least 30 minutes of cooking time for the rice.

Breast of Chicken Val d'Ostina

Serves 4

Tip: To make crumbs, bake French bread in oven at 200 degrees until bread is dry. Cool and grate.

4 boneless chicken breasts, skinned
4 thin slices proscuitto ham
4 thin slices Fontina cheese
½ cup flour
3 eggs, beaten
unseasoned bread crumbs
2 tablespoons olive oil
2 tablespoons butter

Lemon Sauce

¼ cup white wine
1 tablespoon butter
1 lemon, juiced

Pound chicken breasts between wax paper until thin. Lay one slice of proscuitto and one slice of cheese on each breast. Fold over and pat to make "stick." Roll each breast in flour, beaten eggs, and bread crumbs. Place chicken breasts on plate and refrigerate to set coating.

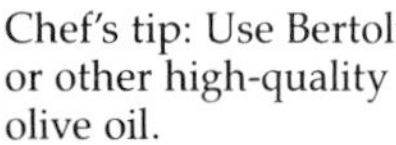

Chef's tip: Use Bertoli or other high-quality olive oil.

In a skillet heat olive oil and butter over high heat until butter foams. Transfer chicken breasts to skillet and immediately lower heat to medium low. Brown for approximately 3 minutes or until done. Remove from skillet and set aside on warm platter.

To prepare Lemon Sauce, pour off all but one-third of oil from skillet and warm over high heat. Add white wine to deglaze pan. Add butter and lemon juice, and cook until reduced by half. Whisk and serve over chicken breasts.

Potato Torta

Serves 10 to 12

4 pounds Idaho potatoes
⅓ cup olive oil
4 large leeks, diced
¼ to ⅓ cup Parmesan cheese, grated
salt and pepper to taste
½ cup (1 stick) butter

Chef's tip: Use Bertoli olive oil or another high-quality brand.

Crust

5 cups flour, sifted
3 eggs, beaten (reserve 1 egg for brushing on crust)
1 cup plus a dash of water

Preheat oven to 450 degrees.

Boil potatoes with skins on, then peel and rice. Set aside. While potatoes are cooking, sauté leeks in olive oil over low heat until soft. Mix potatoes, leeks, cheese, salt, and pepper. Add butter, beating thoroughly. Set aside.

To make crust, mix ingredients together by hand and knead until dough forms a ball and feels "silky." Roll out on pasta machine until thin. Generously oil a 10- × 15-inch baking pan and line with crust, allowing crust to fold over and cover filling. Prick bottom crust. Place filling in pan and fold over crust. Cut slits in top crust and brush top with beaten egg. Place torta in oven, reduce temperature to 375 degrees, and bake for approximately 45 minutes or until golden brown. Remove from oven, turn out onto a cutting board, and cut into serving squares.

Tip: If a pasta machine is not available, divide dough in half and roll out top and bottom as with a pie crust using pan to determine size. Extra flour will facilitate rolling.

Chef's tip: Torta may be served hot or at room temperature.

Spuma de Zambaione

Serves 4 to 6

4 egg yolks
4 tablespoons sugar
½ cup Marsala wine
2 cups (1 pint) heavy cream
2 ounces bittersweet chocolate, grated

In a double boiler cream egg yolks and sugar. Add wine and whisk briskly or use electric mixer on low speed. Heat, stirring continuously until thickened to ribbon consistency. Be careful not to boil. Remove pan from heat and let cool to room temperature.

Whip cream and set aside.

When egg mixture has cooled, fold in whipped cream and grated chocolate, reserving some for garnish. Serve in long-stemmed glasses.

Tip: This is a very rich dessert, so one recipe easily serves 6 people.

Chef's tip: May be kept in refrigerator for several days if covered with plastic wrap.

Ragged Garden Inn
and Restaurant
Sunset Drive,
P.O. Box 1927
Blowing Rock,
North Carolina 28605
704-295-9703

Innkeepers: Joe and Joyce Villani

The Mast Farm Inn

Visiting the Mast Farm Inn is much like going to Grandmother's house, where vegetables come fresh from the garden and the atmosphere is warm and inviting. Innkeepers Francis and Sibyl Pressly, however, are far from the prototypical grandparents of yesteryear. Witty, youthful, and gregarious, the Presslys have lived all over the world, including Brazil, where they were on an assignment for the Peace Corps.

Upon our arrival, Sibyl was gathering flowers for the dinner tables from her garden, with row after neat row brimming with everything from raspberries for cobblers to gourds for decorations. You can sit on the porch in comfortable rockers and watch the afternoon harvest, knowing the dinner menu is in the making. You can even help with the picking if you wish.

The food is served family-style, a welcomed feature when you want seconds of something as good as the sweet potato and apple casserole. Baskets of steaming homemade whole wheat bread emptied within minutes and were quickly replaced with more.

The Mast Farm Inn began as a single log cabin in 1812 and grew to include a blacksmith's shop, barn, springhouse, washhouse, and apple house. The main house was completed in 1885. Then in the early 1900s Finley and Josephine Mast started their inn. They were known far and wide for their fresh food and special down-home hospitality, which has since become a Mast Farm Inn tradition.

We could sense Sibyl's great pride in the restoration of the main house, listed on the National Register of Historic Places as one of the best examples of a self-contained mountain homestead in the North Carolina high country.

After their purchase of the inn in 1984, the Presslys worked side by side with dedicated craftsmen through a bitter winter to restore the house the old-fashioned way. Only authentic tools and construction methods were used. It was a labor of love—and it shows!

Each of the ten guest rooms is named after a member of the Mast family, an important friend, or a former guest. The rooms, many paneled in cherry or chestnut, are furnished with simple, turn-of-the-century antiques. Sibyl's interesting stories give them special personalities.

No trip to the inn is complete without a stop at the Mast General Store, also on the National Register of Historic Places and located near the farm. The antique counters and cases are loaded with merchandise from another time but serve today's customers. The old potbellied stove in the center of the store keeps customers as toasty as it did in the horse-and-buggy days.

Whatever your reason for visiting Valle Crucis—the historic general store, the area's beautiful golf courses, or the scenic back roads—the Mast Farm Inn is a quiet, restful home base for your activities. The Presslys will welcome and pamper you just as Grandmother did years ago.

Chicken with Parsley Dumplings

Serves 8 to 10

Chef's tip: The cooked carrots and peas are for color and taste. Too many peas can sweeten chicken broth too much.

1 quart water
2 teaspoons salt
2 carrots, sliced
1 medium onion, sliced
1 stalk celery, sliced
4- to 5-pound stewing chicken, cut into small pieces
1 cup milk
1/3 cup all-purpose flour
1 cup carrots, diced and cooked
1/2 cup peas, cooked

Dumplings

2 cups all-purpose flour
1 tablespoon baking powder
1 teaspoon salt
1/4 cup fresh parsley, chopped
1/4 cup shortening
1 cup milk

In a saucepan, heat water to boiling and add salt, carrots, onion, celery, and chicken. Simmer chicken until tender. Remove chicken from broth and keep warm. Strain broth and add enough water to make 3 cups. Return broth to saucepan and heat.

Combine milk and flour and mix in blender or shake in a jar. Add slowly to broth, beating with a wire whisk to keep smooth. Cook about 5 minutes and add chicken, diced carrots, and peas.

To make dumplings, sift flour, baking powder, and salt together. Add parsley and cut in shortening. Add milk and mix, stirring as little as possible, to form a soft dough. Drop by tablespoons into chicken soup and simmer 10 minutes uncovered. Cover and simmer for 10 minutes more. Serve immediately.

Chef's tip: Dumpling dough may be frozen and used later.

Tip: If gravy is too rich or thick after the addition of the dumplings, thin with a little chicken broth.

Pork Chop Casserole

Serves 4 to 6

3 medium potatoes, sliced ⅛ inch thick
milk to cover potatoes
6 pork chops, ½ to ¾ inch thick
salt and pepper to taste

Preheat oven to 350 degrees.

Line bottom of baking dish or iron skillet with several layers of sliced potatoes. Season with salt and pepper and cover with milk. Trim fat off pork chops and arrange chops on top of potatoes. Salt and pepper to taste. Bake for 1 to 1½ hours or until pork chops are well cooked but not dry. Serve immediately.

Chef's tip: This is a very simple dish that goes well with garden-fresh vegetables.

Chef's tip: Use potatoes as needed to completely cover bottom of pan. Carefully scrub potatoes so you won't have to peel them.

Chef's tip: If chops begin to brown too quickly, cover loosely with foil.

Vegetable Strudel

Serves 6 to 8

1 head broccoli, diced
2 medium onions, diced
¼ pound carrots, diced
½ pound mushrooms, diced
2 tablespoons olive oil
1 egg, beaten
¼ cup sour cream
¼ cup sherry
¼ cup flour
1 teaspoon black pepper
1 teaspoon fresh dill weed, chopped
1 cup (2 sticks) butter, melted
1-pound package phyllo pastry leaves

Preheat oven to 425 degrees.

Sauté vegetables in olive oil until nearly done and set aside to cool. Combine egg, sour cream, sherry, flour, pepper, and dill weed. Set aside.

Using a pastry brush, grease a 9- × 13-inch baking pan. Divide phyllo leaves into two portions. Carefully spread out a leaf in the pan and brush with melted butter. Place another leaf on top and brush with butter. Repeat until half the leaves are layered.

Spread vegetable filling evenly over dough and pour sour cream mixture over vegetables. Layer remaining leaves on top of filling, brushing each leaf with butter. Bake for 45 minutes or until phyllo is golden brown. Slice and serve immediately.

Tip: Phyllo pastry can usually be found in the refrigerated pastry section of specialty grocery stores. It is also used for making dessert strudels.

Chef's tip: Vegetables can be varied according to availability, but onions and mushrooms are a must. Sugar snap peas are great.

Tip: If phyllo leaves are larger than pan, brush with butter before folding over to fit.

Squash Fritters

Yields 18 small fritters

Tip: Delicate and delicious, these fritters will not overpower any entrée.

2 cups summer squash, grated
½ teaspoon onion, grated
dash of pepper
2 teaspoons sugar
1 teaspoon salt
5 tablespoons flour
2 eggs, beaten
2 teaspoons butter, melted
vegetable oil for frying

Combine all ingredients. Heat griddle and oil. Drop batter by tablespoons onto griddle. Brown on both sides and serve immediately.

Apple and Sweet Potato Casserole

Serves 4 to 6

Tip: This is an excellent dish with poultry or pork.

3 medium sweet potatoes, peeled and sliced
½ cup brown sugar
½ cup pecans, chopped
½ cup (1 stick) butter, softened
4 medium apples, cored and sliced

Tip: This recipe was tested in both a 9- × 13-inch casserole and deep, 9-inch-round baking dish. The shallow casserole made a wonderfully chewy dish.

Preheat oven to 375 degrees.

Butter a casserole dish and line the bottom with half of the sweet potatoes. Combine sugar, pecans, and butter and spread mixture over sweet potatoes. Layer apples over pecan mixture, then add remainder of the sweet potatoes. Cover tightly with foil and bake for 45 minutes or until potatoes are tender. Serve immediately.

Shaker Lemon Pie

Yields one 9-inch pie

4 lemons, peeled
2 cups sugar
4 eggs, beaten
2 9-inch pie shells

Slice peeled lemons as thinly as possible. Remove seeds and soak slices in sugar overnight or at least 2 hours.

Preheat oven to 425 degrees.

Prick bottom of one unbaked pie shell. Add eggs to lemon mixture and pour into pie shell. Top with lattice crust made from second shell. Bake for 15 minutes, reduce heat to 350 degrees, and bake for an additional 40 minutes or until crust is golden brown. Cool and serve.

Chef's tip: This is a very tart pie for real lemon lovers. Quality of lemons makes a difference. If making more than one pie, it is best to mix each filling separately so each pie contains the same number of lemons.

Tip: Avoid overripe lemons with tough membrane.

The Mast Farm Inn
P.O. Box 704
Valle Crucis,
North Carolina 28691
704-963-5857

Innkeepers: Francis and Sibyl Pressly

Eseeola Lodge

Once a year, Grandfather Mountain in the Blue Ridge Mountains comes alive with the sound of Scottish bagpipes. The historic Eseeola Lodge in Linville is the center of the social activities that accompany the games.

The music signals the beginning of the Highland Games and the Gathering of Scottish Clans, when Scots dressed in their tartans and kilts assemble for games, music, and dancing in MacRae Meadow, named in honor of Linville's founding family. It was Hugh MacRae's daughter Agnes, who, as she walked the hillside as a child, envisioned the games that one day would pay homage to her family's strong Scottish heritage. Indeed, this little girl's dream became a reality in the 1950s. The event now attracts over 25,000 visitors a year.

The MacRae family, who came from Scotland to North Carolina in 1770, discovered the area around Grandfather Mountain in 1890 while scouting for coal mines. Impressed with the beauty and quietude, Hugh MacRae and some friends joined together to develop a small resort in Linville. An existing shabby structure became the first inn. It was followed in 1891 by the building of a new inn designed with a wide veranda and a gabled, chimney-topped roof. In the 1920s, a championship golf course was added. Throughout the 1930s the social affairs escalated with fancy dress balls. And the inaugural of Sunday night buffets, where foods from a different country were served, are legendary.

In 1936 the inn burned, causing a considerable loss to generations who had enjoyed the facilities. The remaining Chestnut Annex became the lodge, and additional rooms were added. It was officially renamed Eseeola Lodge. The guest rooms, over fifty years later, seemed unchanged with their traditional chestnut paneling and furnishings. From the private porches, supported by peeled chestnut and poplar logs, guests have views of the lush green lawn bordered with flowers.

Sightseeing is a treat in the Linville area—which is especially noted for Grandfather Mountain Natural Environmental Habitat. Hugh MacRae Morton, owner of Grandfather Mountain and an environmentalist, has brought bears, eagles, and other endangered species for visitors to see.

Many believe Grandfather Mountain received its name because of the one-billion-year-old rock formations. The true story is that pioneers chose the name because, seen from the small village of Foscoe, between Linville and Boone, the mountaintop resembles the profile of an old man gazing at the sky.

The scenery is breathtaking, but the highlight of our stay was Eseeola Lodge. Dining in the richly paneled dining room with waiters in tuxedos offering superb service, we listened to the haunting refrains of Scottish tunes played by an attractive harpist. And as we looked at some of the creative menus, changed daily by chef John Hofland, we only wished we could have extended our stay at Eseeola.

Chilled Smoked Salmon Soup

Serves 4 to 6

1 pound Norwegian smoked salmon
2 cups (1 pint) sour cream
2 cups (1 pint) heavy cream
¼ cup dry white wine
4 tablespoons fresh lemon juice
salt, white pepper, and Tabasco sauce to taste
fresh dill sprigs for garnish

Chef's tip: If soup is too thick, thin with half-and-half.

Puree salmon in a food processor until smooth. Slowly blend in sour cream and heavy cream. Add white wine and remaining ingredients. Chill overnight. Garnish with dill and serve.

Sautéed Medallions of Veal
with Sun-Dried Tomatoes and Sauce Madeira

Serves 4

8 medallions of veal loin, lightly pounded (approximately 3 ounces each)
1 cup all-purpose flour, seasoned with salt and pepper to taste
2 tablespoons clarified butter (or more if needed)

Sauce

3 celery ribs, sliced
1 carrot, sliced
2 onions, coarsely diced
1 shallot, finely diced
¼ cup Madeira wine
2 cups Sauce Espagnole or any good-quality prepared brown sauce
12 black peppercorns, crushed
1 sprig fresh thyme
1 bay leaf
4 ounces sun-dried tomatoes, cut in julienne strips
½ cup (1 stick) cold butter
salt and white pepper to taste

Tip: Sauce Espagnole was not available, so we substituted Saucier Brown Sauce, which was available in the frozen food section of a specialty grocery store.

Tip: Use sun-dried tomatoes preserved in olive oil.

Dredge veal medallions in seasoned flour and pat off any excess. Heat butter in sauté pan over high heat and sauté veal until done. Remove from pan and keep warm on separate platter. Retain drippings for sauce.

Reheat drippings and sauté celery, carrot, onions, and shallot until well browned. Add wine and reduce by half. Add brown sauce, peppercorns, thyme, and bay leaf. Boil briskly, reducing by half again. Strain sauce, return to heat, and add sun-dried tomatoes. Add butter gradually, whisking until melted. Add salt and pepper.

Place hot veal medallions on a platter, cover with julienne tomatoes and sauce. Serve with favorite pasta.

Chef's tip: When sautéing veal, turn medallions when blood beads up on top side. Very hot clarified butter is needed to brown veal properly. The proper temperature is reached when butter first begins to smoke lightly.

Chef's tip: A squeeze of fresh lemon juice can be used to reduce any bitterness in a brown sauce.

Grilled Breast of Chicken
with Tomato Butter Sauce

Serves 4

4 boneless chicken breasts, skinned

Tip: The marinade and sauce recipes yield enough for at least 4 more chicken breasts if desired.

Marinade

¼ cup dry white wine
¼ cup walnut oil
¼ cup vegetable oil
2 tablespoons fresh tarragon, chopped
¼ cup fresh lemon juice
rind of 1 lemon, grated
¼ cup walnuts, coarsely chopped
8 black peppercorns, coarsely ground
1 bay leaf
1 garlic clove, pressed
4 tablespoons soy sauce

Chef's tip: Always take marinated meat out of refrigerator at least 30 minutes before cooking. Cold meat may overcook on the outside before it cooks on the inside.

Sauce

olive oil
12 ripe tomatoes, blanched, peeled, seeded, and diced
2 tablespoons pesto
salt and pepper to taste
1 pound (4 sticks) butter, softened
fresh basil leaves for garnish

Tip: Use Roma tomatoes or small to medium regular tomatoes.

Tip: Prepared pesto can be found in both the refrigerated Italian food section and salad dressing section of specialty food stores.

Combine all marinade ingredients and marinate chicken in refrigerator for 24 hours.

Grill chicken on charcoal grill until done.

To prepare sauce, sauté tomatoes in enough olive oil to keep them from sticking to pan. Add pesto, salt, and pepper. Cook tomatoes until most of the liquid is evaporated. Puree mixture in blender or food processor. Strain and return to saucepan. Heat and whisk in butter gradually until completely melted. Adjust seasonings. Ladle sauce onto warm plate, place chicken breast on top, and garnish with fresh basil leaves.

Chef's tip: Coals should be very hot for grilling chicken. Coals should be gray with ash with an occasional red flame. You should not be able to hold your hand 6 inches above coals for more than 3 seconds.

Poached Florida Snapper
with Béarnaise Sauce, Almonds, and Grapes

Serves 4

4 snapper fillets, skinned and boned (approximately 6 ounces each)
4 tablespoons fresh lemon juice
2 shallots, finely diced
½ cup (1 stick) butter
salt and pepper to taste
2 cups dry white wine
1 cup almonds, sliced, sautéed in butter, and lightly salted
1 cup seedless white grapes, peeled (or canned)

Tip: If using fresh grapes, allow enough time to peel them.

Sauce

2½ tablespoons dry white wine
2½ tablespoons shallots, finely diced
2½ tablespoons tarragon vinegar
2 teaspoons parsley stems, chopped
8 white peppercorns
3 egg yolks
1¼ cups clarified butter, warmed
salt to taste
pinch of cayenne pepper
½ teaspoon lemon juice
½ teaspoon fresh tarragon leaves, chopped
1 teaspoon parsley leaves, chopped
lemon wedges and tarragon leaves for garnish

Tip: To clarify butter, place butter in a saucepan over moderate heat until melted. Reduce heat and skim off any foam. Cook on low heat until milky solids collect on the bottom of pan and liquid is clear. Strain out residue.

Chef's tip: When making Béarnaise Sauce, always use clarified butter that is warm but not hot—hot butter will separate the sauce. Test by holding your finger in the butter for 10 seconds. If it's too hot, you'll be unable to do this for more than a few seconds.

Chef's tip: If Béarnaise Sauce starts to separate after cooking, try one of the following methods to bring it back: (1) Whisk one ice cube into sauce until melted; (2) add a few drops of boiling water or vinegar; (3) place 2 tablespoons of boiling water in a clean mixing bowl and whisk in separated sauce. Whisk slowly and constantly until sauce is smooth once again.

Preheat oven to 350 degrees.

Place snapper fillets in a buttered baking dish. Cover with lemon juice, shallots, and dots of butter. Add salt, pepper, and white wine. Cover with foil and bake for 10 to 15 minutes or until fish is just cooked. Remove from oven and keep warm.

To prepare sauce, combine wine, shallots, vinegar, parsley stems, and peppercorns. Cook over medium heat until reduced by two-thirds. Strain through cheesecloth or fine mesh strainer.

Combine egg yolks and reduced liquid in a stainless steel mixing bowl placed over a pot of boiling water. Stir briskly with wire whisk until mixture is the consistency of thick cream. Gradually add clarified butter, whipping constantly. Add remaining ingredients and mix well. Hold at warm temperature over water bath.

Place each fillet on a plate and pour sauce across the center. Arrange almonds on each end of fillet, with a row of grapes across front of fish. Garnish with lemon wedges and fresh tarragon.

Roast Loin of Pork
with Applejack Brandy Sauce

Serves 4 to 6

4-pound pork loin, trimmed of fat and bone
1 cup apples, peeled, cored, and sliced
1 cup walnuts, coarsely chopped
1 cup raisins
3 cloves garlic, peeled and crushed
8 black peppercorns, crushed
salt and pepper to taste

Sauce

clarified butter or vegetable oil
3 stalks celery, sliced
1 carrot, sliced
1 onion, coarsely diced
1 shallot, finely diced
1 sprig fresh thyme
1 bay leaf
2 cloves garlic, minced
6 black peppercorns, crushed
1 fresh apple, cored and chopped
¼ cup applejack brandy or Calvados
2 cups brown sauce (Sauce Espagnole)
½ cup (1 stick) butter
salt and pepper to taste
fresh apple slices for garnish

Preheat oven to 500 degrees.

Use a steel knife sharpener to pierce a hole lengthwise through the center of the pork loin. A long thin knife can be used to widen hole to approximately 1 inch in diameter.

Stuff hole with apples, raisins, and walnuts, alternating in equal parts until loin is fully stuffed. Rub outside of pork with garlic, salt, and pepper. Bake at 225 degrees until internal temperature reaches 165 degrees on meat thermometer.

To prepare sauce, coat the bottom of a saucepan with clarified butter or vegetable oil. Brown the celery, carrot, onion, and shallot. Add seasoning and apples and sauté 3 minutes more. Add brandy and reduce by two-thirds. Add brown sauce and boil briskly until reduced by half. Strain, return sauce to heat, and whisk in butter gradually until melted. Add salt and pepper to taste.

Ladle sauce onto warm plate and place two slices of pork loin over sauce. Garnish with fresh apple slices.

Tip: Sauce Espagnole was not available, so we substituted Saucier Brown Sauce, which was available in the frozen food section at a specialty grocery store.

Chef's tip: For best results place pork loin in a very hot oven (500 degrees) and sear outside of roast. Turn roast to brown on all sides, then reduce heat to 225 degrees, cover roast with foil, and cook slowly until done. Roast will retain all juices when cooked in this manner.

Lemon Squares

Yields one 13- × 9-inch pastry

Tip: Press dough into pan gently to keep crust tender and easier to cut. A serrated knife can be used for cutting squares.

1 cup (2 sticks) butter or margarine
1 cup confectioners' sugar, sifted
2 cups all-purpose flour, sifted

Topping

4 eggs, beaten
2 cups sugar
⅓ cup lemon juice
½ teaspoon baking powder
¼ cup all-purpose flour
confectioners' sugar for garnish

Preheat oven to 350 degrees.

Cream butter; add flour and sugar. Mix until dough sticks together. Grease a 9- × 13-inch baking pan and press dough into bottom. Bake for 20 to 25 minutes or until golden.

Beat eggs and sugar; add remaining ingredients and mix thoroughly. Pour over baked crust and bake about 25 minutes or until light brown.

Chill overnight. Cut into squares and sprinkle with confectioners' sugar before serving.

Eseeola Lodge

Hummingbird Cake

Yields one 3-layer cake

1½ cups oil
3 eggs, beaten
1½ teaspoons vanilla
8-ounce can crushed pineapple, undrained
2 bananas, mashed
2 cups sugar
1 teaspoon salt
3 cups all-purpose flour, sifted
1 teaspoon baking soda
1½ teaspoons cinnamon

Icing

8 ounces cream cheese, softened
½ cup (1 stick) butter, softened
16-ounce box confectioners' sugar
½ cup walnuts, chopped

Preheat oven to 350 degrees.

Combine all wet ingredients. Add all dry ingredients and mix until moist. Grease and flour three 9-inch cake pans. Divide batter equally among pans. Bake about 25 to 30 minutes or until done. Cool on racks.

To prepare icing, mix cream cheese and butter. Add sugar and mix thoroughly. Spread icing between layers, ice top and sides, then sprinkle top with chopped walnuts. Serve.

Note: This cake was especially created for the Scottish Games, held each year at nearby Grandfather Mountain.

Eseeola Lodge
P.O. Box 98
Linville, North Carolina
28646
704-733-4311

General Manager:
John M. Blackburn

The Grove Park Inn

Asheville, home of the renowned Grove Park Inn, enjoys a mystique bestowed by those who have lived there, visited, and even written about it. When city fathers banned Thomas Wolfe's *Look Homeward, Angel,* Asheville achieved an infamy that brought visitors from the world over to this rustic mountain haven. When F. Scott and Zelda Fitzgerald stayed at the Grove Park Inn, the inn's fame was sealed.

As early as 1830 Asheville enjoyed a reputation as a popular mountain resort. When Edwin Wiley Grove came from St. Louis to relocate his drug company, what he discovered was a climate so beneficial to his health that he decided to build a resort overlooking Sunset Mountain, which he loved.

The huge boulders of the inn's main building came from Sunset Mountain and surrounding areas. Italian stonemasons and hundreds of local workmen fitted the stones together so that only the natural, weathered face of the stone was visible. Solid steel and concrete reinforcing reflected Mr. Grove's desire that the inn be "built not

for the present alone, but for ages to come, and the admiration of generations yet unborn." In 1973 the Grove Park Inn received National Historic Landmark status.

Over the years, the Grove Park Inn has built an impressive reputation and served many illustrious patrons, beginning with William Jennings Bryan's address at ceremonies to open the inn on July 1, 1913. In 1955 the inn was purchased by Charles A. Sammons of Dallas, Texas. Under Mr. Sammons's farsighted development, the original structure has been completely renovated and two wings added.

These major new structures plus the golf course, tennis courts, health club facilities, swimming pools, and conference facilities allow the Grove Park Inn to enjoy the best of two worlds. The inn today is where history lives in its wonderfully restored main building and many original furnishings from the Arts and Crafts Period of 1900 to 1916 by such notables as William Morris and Roycrofters. And yet all the modern amenities and conveniences are there, too.

Six different restaurants also assure just the right style of dining. The Sunset Terrace—with its namesake view, friendly service, entertainment, and, of course, the food—was our favorite. Executive chef Michael Villa plans menus and supervises the staff, which totals nearly 250 members for all six restaurants. With his extensive experience at many of the largest hotels and restaurants from coast to coast, Villa makes guiding the variety of dining experiences at the Grove Park Inn seem easy.

For all its grandness, the Grove Park Inn can be quiet, relaxing, and personal—a place where, in spite of its world-class resort status, you can get away for a refreshing walk alone, sit in a Kennedy rocker and watch the sun burn the mist off the greens in the morning, or snuggle up around the fireplace on cool evenings.

Bisque of Clam and Chicken

Serves 8

¼ cup (½ stick) butter
¼ cup flour
2 cups clam juice
1 cup chicken stock
1 cup half-and-half
1 cup heavy cream
¼ cup onion, finely chopped
¼ cup celery, diced
½ cup chicken, diced
½ cup clams, diced
salt and pepper to taste

Melt butter and stir in flour. Add clam juice and chicken stock, stirring constantly. Bring to a boil. Add half-and-half, heavy cream, onions, celery, chicken, and clams. Stir thoroughly and let simmer for 20 to 30 minutes. Add salt and pepper and serve immediately.

Stuffed Mountain Trout

Serves 8

4 pounds fresh trout

Tip: Number of servings depends on size of trout.

Stuffing

½ pound shrimp, peeled, deveined, and chopped
½ pound haddock, poached and flaked
2 tablespoons onion, minced
2 tablespoons chives, minced
2 cups garlic bread, diced in small pieces
3 egg yolks
1 cup (½ pint) heavy cream
½ teaspoon Old Bay Seafood Seasoning
½ teaspoon Worcestershire sauce
1 teaspoon dry mustard
salt and pepper to taste
2 tablespoons lemon juice
1 cup flour
4 tablespoons olive oil

Garnish

¼ pound (½ cup) almonds, slivered
2 tablespoons butter
lemon juice to taste
fresh parsley, chopped

Preheat oven to 375 degrees.

Clean trout and trim off fins. Remove backbone, but do not cut through back skin. Set aside.

Grind together shrimp, haddock, onions, chives, and bread using a food grinder or chopper. Add egg yolks and heavy cream slowly until absorbed. Add seasonings and lemon juice.

Fill trout with stuffing. Bind together with string. Roll in flour and fry in olive oil until golden brown on each side.

Transfer trout to a baking dish, cover with foil, and bake for 10 minutes. Remove foil and bake an additional 5 minutes.

To prepare garnish, sauté almonds in butter until brown, add lemon juice and parsley. Pour over fish and serve.

Tip: To remove backbone, use a small, sharp knife and cut the underside of the fish all the way to the tail. Hold the fish open and nick the membrane to expose each rib. Slide the knife blade under the ribs to lift them free of the flesh. Snap ribs off backbone with your fingers. To free the backbone, open the fish as wide as possible, and run the knife down both sides of backbone, being careful not to cut through the skin. With a pair of kitchen scissors, sever the backbone as close to the head as possible. Pull the bone up, working toward the tail, and sever as close to the tail as possible.

The Grove Park Inn
290 Macon Avenue
Asheville,
North Carolina 28804
704-252-2711

General Manager:
Herman R. von Treskow

Pisgah View Ranch

Innkeeper Ruby Cogburn's family, the Davises, have held the original land grant for Pisgah View Ranch since 1790, when the territory was first opened for settlement. The stories and traditions from its long history have become rich and abundant.

When visiting the ranch, be sure to look for the large mound of boulders. The Davises hid their precious meat supply under the stones during the Civil War to keep it safe from Yankees.

The original ranch building, built in 1790, now houses a museum. The main ranch house dates back 115 years but did not become a boardinghouse until the turn of the century. Mrs. Cogburn can still remember the traveling dentist who would set up his chair on the front porch and tend to all the neighbors' dental needs. As a child, she would run upstairs and hide under the bed until he left.

The barn where Ruby Cogburn played in the hayloft and watched the cows being milked has been remodeled and converted to an entertainment hall where an award-winning square dance team performs clogging routines. This is an extraordinary sight for anyone who has never experienced this vigorous dance form. Guests are invited to join the dancing.

Phyllis Parris, Mrs. Cogburn's daughter, who along with her husband Sam helps run Pisgah View Ranch, also has her stories about growing up on the ranch. Friendly and helpful, Phyllis likes to share the anecdotes about the ranch, her family, and guests, which she has collected over the years.

Pisgah View Ranch has grown one bedroom or one cabin at a time. Today there are twenty-two cabins in all, many large enough for an entire family. There are fifty bedrooms, including those in the main ranch house. From the days when people walked in the pastures and sat in rocking chairs for entertainment, the ranch has grown to include such activities as swimming, fishing in the trout-stocked pond, shuffleboard, table tennis, horseback riding, and hiking the many trails on the ranch's 1,700 acres. The ranch is also within a few minutes' drive of many area attractions, such as the Biltmore House and the Thomas Wolfe Memorial. You can climb Pisgah Mountain, named for one of the peaks Moses saw in Jordan on his forty-year journey to the Promised Land, or you can view it from the comfort of one of the rockers on the front porch.

Every year more improvements take place. The A-frame cabin in the woods recently acquired a new bathroom with whirlpool bath and a new deck; Chickadee Cabin has a new bedroom.

As the years go by, Pisgah View Ranch seems to evolve further into an outstanding family vacation place. Where else can you find clean mountain air, plenty of vigorous activities, wholesome entertainment, a sense of history, and good old Southern desserts like oatmeal, vinegar, and buttermilk pies?

Dinner Rolls

Yields three dozen rolls

Note: This is an excellent and easy homestyle dinner roll recipe.

1 cup milk, warmed
¼ cup sugar
1 teaspoon salt
¼ cup (½ stick) margarine, melted
2 tablespoons yeast
½ cup warm water
2 eggs, beaten
5½ cups all-purpose flour

Preheat oven to 375 to 400 degrees.

Mix milk, sugar, and salt in a very large bowl. Add margarine and set aside.

Dissolve yeast in warm water and then add to milk mixture. Add eggs and mix well. Add flour until dough is stiff.

Grease top of dough and allow to rise in a warm place until double in volume. Knead dough down, put into greased muffin pans, and let rise again until almost double. Bake about 25 minutes or until golden brown.

Buttermilk Pie

Yields one 10-inch pie

Note: Testers considered this pie an award-winner.

3 eggs
1¼ cups sugar
6 tablespoons (¾ stick) margarine, melted
1 cup buttermilk
1 teaspoon vanilla
1 heaping tablespoon flour
½ teaspoon lemon flavoring
10-inch pie shell, unbaked

Preheat oven to 450 degrees.

Combine all ingredients and pour into the unbaked pie shell. Bake at 450 degrees for 10 minutes, reduce temperature to 350 degrees, and bake about 35 minutes more or until done. Cool and serve.

Oatmeal Pie

Yields one 10-inch pie

½ cup (1 stick) margarine
2 eggs, beaten
⅔ cup dark corn syrup
⅔ cup sugar
⅔ cup oatmeal
1 teaspoon vanilla
10-inch pie shell, unbaked

Note: Try this pie. It is outstanding.

Preheat oven to 325 degrees.

Blend all ingredients in the order listed. Pour into pie shell and bake for about 40 minutes or until done. Cool and serve.

Vinegar Pie

Yields two 10-inch pies

1½ cups (3 sticks) margarine, melted
3¾ cups sugar
9 eggs, beaten
6 tablespoons vinegar
1 tablespoon flour
9 tablespoons milk
1 tablespoon vanilla
2 unbaked pie shells

Note: As strange as it sounds, this pie tastes great.

Preheat oven to 350 degrees.

Combine ingredients in the order listed, mixing thoroughly. Pour into the two uncooked pie shells and bake about 35 minutes or until done. Cool and serve.

Tip: Pie is done when crust is golden and filling becomes firm.

Note: A very good, very light cake.

Carrot-Pineapple Cake

Yields one 9- × 13-inch cake

1½ cups vegetable oil
2 cups sugar
3 eggs, beaten
1 cup crushed pineapple, drained
2 cups carrots, grated
2½ cups all-purpose flour
1 teaspoon baking soda
1 teaspoon cinnamon
½ teaspoon salt
1 teaspoon vanilla
1 cup nuts, chopped

Icing

½ cup (1 stick) margarine, softened
3 ounces cream cheese, softened
1 pound confectioners' sugar, sifted
1 teaspoon vanilla

Preheat oven to 350 degrees.

Cream oil and sugar together. Add eggs, pineapple, and carrots. Sift together flour, soda, cinnamon, and salt. Mix with pineapple mixture. Add vanilla and nuts, mixing thoroughly. Bake in a greased 9- × 13-inch pan for about 45 minutes or until done. Cool slightly.

To prepare icing, cream margarine and cream cheese together. Add sugar, mixing thoroughly, then add vanilla. Make sure icing is smooth. Ice cake and serve.

Grandma's Apple Cake

Yields one 9-inch-square cake

Note: This cake was moist and light.

1 cup sugar
1½ cups flour
1 teaspoon baking soda
½ teaspoon salt
½ cup shortening
1 egg, beaten
4 cups apples, peeled, cored, and chopped
2 teaspoons vanilla

Topping

2 teaspoons flour
2 teaspoons cinnamon or vanilla
2 teaspoons butter, melted
¾ cup brown sugar

Preheat oven to 350 degrees.

Sift together sugar, flour, soda, and salt. Set aside.

Cream shortening and add egg. Add apples and vanilla and combine with dry ingredients. Mix thoroughly and pour into a 9-inch-square baking pan.

To prepare topping, mix all ingredients together and pour on top of cake. Bake for 30 to 40 minutes or until done. Serve warm or cold.

Pumpkin Cake

Yields one 9- × 13-inch cake

Note: This cake was loved by everyone who tasted it.

½ teaspoon cinnamon
½ teaspoon cloves
1 teaspoon baking soda
¼ teaspoon baking powder
¾ teaspoon salt
1½ cups sugar
1 cup flour
½ cup vegetable oil
½ cup water
1 cup pumpkin, cooked and mashed
2 eggs, beaten

Tip: Canned pumpkin can be substituted for fresh pumpkin.

Preheat oven to 350 degrees.

Combine all dry ingredients, then add oil and water and mix well. Add pumpkin and eggs, mix well, and pour into a greased 9- × 13-inch pan. Bake for at least 35 minutes or until done. Serve warm or cold.

Pisgah View Ranch
Route 1
Candler, North Carolina
28715
704-667-9100

Innkeeper:
Ruby Cogburn

The Swag Country Inn

Time alone stands still at the Swag Country Inn. Everything else seems to be in a constant state of evolution. Surely regulars to this mountain meadow retreat must wonder what Dan and Deener Matthews have been up to this year to increase the comfort and pleasure of inn guests.

No task seems to be too great for this indefatigable couple, who now live in New York City during the off-season from November through April.

The Matthewses purchased the original 250 acres in 1969. For as long as their mountain neighbors can recall, this particular site, a dip between two knolls on a high ridge, has been known as "the Swag." The inn sits where a farmer once grew potatoes and hauled them down to market on a mule-drawn sled.

The grade to the inn site was far too steep for motorized vehicles, but with the help of three bulldozers, a dynamite crew, and 150 truckloads of gravel, the two-and-a-half-mile driveway was completed in three months.

No ordinary logs would do to construct the Matthews's private retreat. The entire family searched the countryside for old log buildings. It took over a year and a half to find, dismantle, and relocate the six log structures that were used for the inn. One cabin dated back to 1795; another was an old church, which is now the cathedral-ceilinged living room. For the sake of authenticity, the huge fireplace at the far end of the room had to be constructed without mortar using surface stones from dry riverbeds and not from quarried stone.

Dan, who did all the design work, sacrificed authenticity for aesthetics to design the extra large windows in the living room. What a shame it would have been to lose the grand vistas and the glorious early-morning sunlight that streams in.

Recently Deener added coffee mills and coffee makers to each room—"so guests can have their first cup of coffee in the privacy of their own porch," she explained. There are twelve rooms in all at the inn. Eight have private porches and refrigerators; five have steam showers with built-in benches; two have whirlpool baths; and two suites have sleeping lofts that are perfect for children or teenagers. An underground playroom has a racketball/volleyball court.

New additions outdoors include a two-and-a-half-mile nature trail marked for local flora. The trail is a distinct contrast to the rugged trails into the Great Smoky Mountains National Park, which begins only twenty feet away. The soothing swimming pond now has a black walnut boat in addition to the hammock and gazebo.

The food itself also improves constantly. Because many guests are concerned about calories and cholesterol, Deener is careful with the menu. "We've gone to great lengths to lower or eliminate cholesterol without sacrificing the quality of our dishes," she explained. The Swag serves three meals a day to guests as well as dinner to the public by reservation. Guests who wish to spend the day hiking or climbing among the azaleas, mountain laurel, rhododenron, and wild flowers can request to have a picnic lunch. Otherwise there's nothing like a friendly lunch served family-style, followed by a little rocking on the porch or sunbathing in the meadow or high up on the knoll, where another group of chairs overlooks the breathtaking Cataloochee Valley.

Low-Cholesterol Orange Muffins

Yields 18 large muffins or three dozen small muffins

Chef's tip: Deener Matthews recommends I Can't Believe It's Not Butter and Vegelene cooking spray for their taste and low-cholesterol benefits.

Chef's tip: Lemons can be substituted for oranges.

Chef's tip: Bake large muffins 20 minutes, small muffins 15 minutes. Deener prefers the small muffins because people can have two or three without feeling too full. The smaller ones also present very nicely.

1 cup (2 sticks) butter-margarine spread
¾ cup sugar
2 eggs
1 teaspoon baking soda
1 cup lowfat buttermilk
2 cups all-purpose flour
rind of 2 oranges, grated
nonstick cooking spray

Preheat oven to 375 degrees.

Cream "butter" and sugar. Add eggs and beat until smooth. Add baking soda to buttermilk and combine with egg mixture. Add flour but mix only enough to moisten. Add orange rind.

Spray muffin pans with nonstick cooking spray. Fill cups two-thirds full and bake for 20 minutes or until done. Remove from tins and serve.

Low-Cholesterol Herb Bread

Serves 6 to 8

½ cup butter-margarine spread or margarine
1 teaspoon parsley flakes
½ teaspoon Italian seasoning
¼ teaspoon dill weed
1 clove garlic
14-ounce loaf Italian or French bread

Preheat oven to 350 degrees.

Combine "butter" and seasonings in blender or processor. Slice bread into ½-inch thick slices and place in foil. Spread each slice with herb mixture and form back into loaf. Spread remaining herb mixture on top of loaf. Close foil and bake for about 20 minutes. Serve immediately.

Chef's tip: This bread freezes well.

Low-Cholesterol Indian-Style Chicken

Serves 4

4 chicken breast halves, skinned and boned
1 cup (8 ounces) plain lowfat yogurt
½ teaspoon curry powder
½ teaspoon paprika
½ package (1½ ounces) pickled ginger, chopped
⅓ teaspoon cardamon
nonstick cooking spray
2 tablespoons Major Gray's chutney

Marinate chicken in yogurt and all seasonings for 24 hours.

Preheat oven to 350 degrees.

Spray baking pan with nonstick cooking spray. Arrange chicken in pan and bake for 20 to 30 minutes or until done. Remove and arrange on platter with a dollop of chutney per serving.

Pork Loin
with Currant Wine Sauce

Serves 12 to 18

6 to 9 pounds lean boneless pork loin
seasoned salt
garlic powder

Chef's tip: This sauce can also be served over ham or poultry.

Sauce

1 cup red currant jelly
6-ounce can orange juice, undiluted
1 tablespoon Worcestershire sauce
½ teaspoon dry mustard

Chef's tip: Use a quick-probe meat thermometer to test temperature. The roast can be left in oven at 150 degrees until serving.

Chef's tip: For brighter color, add 2 drops of red food color.

Preheat oven to 350 degrees.

Sprinkle seasoned salt and garlic powder on roast. Bake until interior temperature of roast reaches 160 degrees.

To make sauce, combine all ingredients and heat slowly until jelly melts and mixture is thoroughly heated. Do not boil. Puree in blender until smooth. Serve warm over pork roast.

Hot Vegetable Salad

Serves 4 to 6

3 medium yellow squash, sliced
3 medium onions, halved and sliced
3 medium tomatoes, peeled and sliced
3 medium zucchini, sliced
Italian seasoning
olive oil
¼ cup Parmesan cheese, grated
¼ cup Monterey Jack cheese, grated

Chef's tip: Number of people served is determined by the quantity of vegetables used. This dish can be made as large or small as desired.

Preheat oven to 325 degrees.

In a large baking dish, layer each of the vegetables, drizzling olive oil and sprinkling Parmesan cheese and Italian seasoning on each layer in gentle amounts just for flavor. Top with Monterey Jack cheese and remaining Parmesan cheese. Cover with foil and bake about 30 minutes. Uncover for the last 10 minutes to brown lightly on top. Serve immediately.

Chef's tip: Vegetables will be crisp but tender enough to cut with a dinner fork.

Chef's tip: If there are any leftovers from this dish, they are perfect for a soup the next day when put through a food processor.

The Swag Country Inn
Box 280A, Route 2,
Hemphill Road
Waynesville,
North Carolina 28786
704-926-0430,
704-926-9978

Innkeepers: Deener and Dan Matthews

Cataloochee Ranch

In the early 1930s a young forester by the name of Tom Alexander was already taking stout-hearted adventure-seekers to experience the rugged beauty of the Great Smoky Mountains. He would pitch tents for them, provide food for them, and arrange horses for transportation. From this beginning grew a tradition for hospitality that can still be enjoyed at Cataloochee Ranch.

Tom Alexander's daughters, Judy Coker and Alice Aumen, along with Alice's husband Tom and other family members, still run the inn, which also serves a working cattle and sheep ranch located on a thousand serene and picturesque acres in Maggie Valley.

One of the special amenities still available at Cataloochee Ranch is a three- or six-day trail ride into the 500,000-acre Great Smoky Mountains National Park. Some nights are spent in tents; horses still provide the transportation; but there is one big difference: the food. A chuck wagon now brings everything from fresh vegetables from the ranch garden to a reflector oven for making fresh bread.

Meanwhile, at the main ranch house a fire is usually crackling in the huge fireplace, and guests are reading in the overstuffed armchairs or walking outside in the dew-covered fields. Breakfast includes thick, crispy Cataloochee toast and warm honey.

Unlike most of the inns of North Carolina, Cataloochee Ranch stays open year-round. From spring through fall, accommodations include rooms in the main ranch house or in separate one- or two-bedroom log cabins that surround the fish pond. Each cabin has its own stack of firewood and rockers on the porch. Inside, the rustic log walls contrast with the lace curtains, cozy quilts, and antique furnishings. The new Silver Belle Ski Lodge, recently opened to accommodate the winter crowds from the nearby Cataloochee Ski Area, was designed to duplicate the original, weathered log construction of the ranch's older buildings.

Although our visit occurred in the early fall, when the leaves were beginning to change colors and the morning air was crisp and invigorating, every season has its distinct pleasures at Cataloochee Ranch. Winter, of course, blends the solitude of snow-covered hillsides with the exhilaration of snow sports. In spring, we were told, the valley is covered with a blanket of lush, tender grass and wild flowers. Summer is the action season, filled with riding, hiking, tennis, horseshoe pitching, swimming, and fishing.

Whatever the time of year, take a sweater, a good book, and only casual apparel. Cataloochee Ranch offers all the action and relaxation anyone could ever ask for.

Old-Fashioned Spoon Bread

Serves 5 to 6

Chef's tip: Spoon bread is especially good with baked country ham and red-eye gravy. If any is left over, slice and fry it the next morning.

1 cup cornmeal
2 cups water
1 tablespoon margarine
½ teaspoon salt
1 egg, beaten
1 cup milk

Preheat oven to 325 degrees.

Combine cornmeal, water, margarine, and salt in a saucepan and cook over medium heat, stirring frequently, until thick. Remove from heat. Beat egg and milk together and add to cornmeal mixture. Pour into a greased 1-quart casserole and bake about 45 minutes. Serve by the spoonfuls.

Frybread

Serves 5 to 6

Chef's tip: For an entirely different bread, substitute flour for cornmeal and add 1 tablespoon baking powder and 1 tablespoon shortening.

1 cup cornmeal
½ teaspoon salt
1 cup milk
oil to ½-inch depth in pan

Mix cornmeal, salt, and milk. Drop by spoonfuls into hot oil. Brown on both sides, drain on paper towels, and serve.

Cataloochee Puff Toast

Serves 8

1 loaf bread
2 cups flour
4 teaspoons baking powder
½ cup sugar
pinch of salt
½ teaspoon cinnamon
½ teaspoon nutmeg
1 egg, beaten
1 teaspoon vanilla
1½ cups milk
2 teaspoons oil
oil for deep-frying (approximately 2 cups)
confectioners' sugar
syrup or honey

Cut bread in diagonal, ¾-inch slices and spread out to dry overnight.

Combine flour, baking powder, sugar, salt, spices, egg, vanilla, milk, and two tablespoons oil to make a thick batter. Heat enough oil to deep-fry. Coat each piece of bread in the batter and fry until golden and crisp. Drain on paper towels.

Sprinkle with confectioners' sugar and serve immediately with syrup or warm honey.

Note: There is much discussion on the origin of this recipe, a favorite Sunday brunch item at Cataloochee Ranch. It is thought to be French, but Norman, the ranch chef for twenty years, added most of the spices.

Mountain Candy Roaster Puff

Serves 4

1½ cups Candy Roaster, cooked and mashed
1 tablespoon butter
⅓ cup sugar
salt to taste
dash of lemon juice
1 egg, beaten
½ teaspoon vanilla
½ teaspoon nutmeg
1 teaspoon cinnamon
1 cup milk

Preheat oven to 325 degrees.

Mash Candy Roaster with butter. Mix with all remaining ingredients in order listed. Pour into a greased 1-quart casserole and bake 45 minutes or until done. Serve immediately with country ham or poultry.

Note: A Candy Roaster is a member of the pumpkin family, but has a much more delicate flavor and does not have the stringy texture. It is indigenous to the Great Smoky Mountains area and comes in all shapes, sizes, and colors—from an ugly and warty green to a gorgeous orange hue. Cut up into chunks, it freezes very well. No blanching is necessary.

Chef's tip: Sweet potatoes or butternut or acorn squash can also be used in this recipe.

Tip: One small pumpkin will yield about 1½ cups. Remove seeds, chop into large chunks, and cook in a small amount of water about 30 minutes. Cool, remove skin, and mash.

Corn in the Husk

Serves 6

6 ears fresh corn, unhusked
3 teaspoons butter or margarine
2 teaspoons salt

Gently pull back husk on each ear and remove silk. Insert butter and replace husk around ear. Add salt to enough water to cover ears of corn. Soak about 30 minutes. Drain and cook on charcoal grill, turning frequently. Grill about 30 minutes or until done. Serve in husk.

Chef's tip: Corn and steak or other main dish can be cooked on the grill at the same time for a simple, delicious camp dinner.

Baked Country Ham
and Red-Eye Gravy

Serves 30

1 country ham (18 pounds with bone in)
1 cup vinegar
water
brown sugar
ground cloves
¼ to ½ cup strong coffee

Preheat oven to 325 degrees.

Soak ham in a large pot for 24 hours covered with vinegar and water. Drain and cover ham with fresh water and simmer for 3 hours. Cool enough to trim off excess fat and stronger ham on underside. Score ham and rub well with brown sugar and ground cloves. Place ham in a roaster with rack and bake uncovered for about 30 minutes. Slice very thin.

To make gravy, pour off all drippings and add coffee to roaster. Warm over medium heat, deglazing pan juices. Serve with country ham.

Tip: Country ham provides more servings than a regular ham because of its saltiness, which calls for thin slices.

Tip: Bear can be special-ordered through some specialty butcher shops or through wild-game suppliers who ship overnight.

Bear Roast

Serves 6 to 8

1 lemon, juiced
salt and pepper to taste
garlic, chopped
herbs of choice
4-pound bear roast
½ cup water
garlic salt
1 teaspoon celery seed
½ teaspoon oregano
½ teaspoon thyme
½ teaspoon basil
salt and pepper to taste

Chef's tip: This recipe is also good for venison.

Marinate roast overnight in lemon juice, salt, pepper, garlic, and herbs.

Preheat oven to 325 degrees.

Sear all sides of roast in a heavy pot. Add water, garlic salt, celery seed, oregano, thyme, basil, salt, and pepper. Cover and cook in oven slowly about 3 hours or until tender. Drain drippings, skim off fat, and serve.

Blackberry Cobbler

Yields one 8-inch-square cobbler

1 quart (4 cups) fresh or frozen blackberries
1 cup sugar
4 tablespoons cornstarch
½ cup (1 stick) margarine, melted

Pastry

¼ cup shortening
1½ cups flour, sifted
dash of salt
4 to 6 tablespoons ice water
1 egg, beaten

Preheat oven to 400 degrees.

Combine sugar, cornstarch, and margarine. Toss with blackberries and pour into an 8-inch-square baking dish.

To prepare pastry, cream shortening and add flour, salt, and ice water. Mix with pastry cutter or fork until crumbly but moist enough to hold together when rolled. Add more water if necessary. Roll out very thin and cut into ½-inch strips. Arrange lattice strips over berries. Brush with egg and bake about 45 minutes or until golden brown. Serve warm or cold.

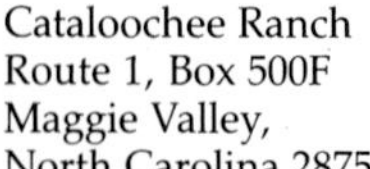

Cataloochee Ranch
Route 1, Box 500F
Maggie Valley,
North Carolina 28751
704-926-1401

Innkeepers:
Alice Aumen and
Judy Coker

Fryemont Inn

Being an innkeeper requires stamina, perseverance, a sense of humor, patience, and a willingness to share one's life with the world. Ask Sue and George Brown, owners of the Fryemont Inn in Bryson City since 1982.

By six o'clock on the morning of our arrival, George was already up prepping the oversize charcoal grill where he would soon cook a 150-pound pig. Some 125 people—inn guests and Bryson City residents—were coming for a Pig Pickin', a twice-yearly event that also includes live country music and plenty of fun long into the night.

Early the next morning this intrepid couple were back up early to say good-bye to departing guests and supervise the staff that maintains the inn—with its thirty-seven rooms and four suites on the pine-tree-covered grounds. Very late that evening we noticed George was still in his office doing the day's bookkeeping.

Sue Brown continues to serve the simple country fare that guests have come to

expect from Fryemont Inn. The Cheese Soup and Mushroom Business recipes were actually passed down from the original owner, Captain Amos Frye, who completed the inn in 1923. Frye had made his fortune as a lumber baron, but when times got tough he decided to build an inn using the best chestnut, oak, and maple he could find. The exterior shingles were cut from huge poplars and are so durable they still add their deep color and rustic texture to the main structure. The most skillful blacksmith from that time, John Carson, forged the ornamental hardware. Furnishings for the inn were locally produced in virgin cherry and walnut woods. Cherokee stonemasons built the huge fireplaces, which can accommodate eight-foot logs.

Some say the Fryemont was designed by Richard Hunt, who designed the Biltmore House in Asheville. There are still people around who were alive when the Biltmore House was being built, and they concur that the same architect built both. But Sue says Hunt died before the Fryemont was built. Even so, some connection must exist because of the unusual "pocket" windows that slide into recesses in the walls of both structures. The Browns' research suggests that the same supervising site architect may have been on hand for the building of both. The inn is listed in the National Register of Historic Places.

Besides knowing all the local lore, the Browns are well versed in what their region offers for entertainment and action. Within minutes of the Fryemont there is hiking, fishing, tubing, biking, and rafting down the Nantahala Gorge. The Oconaluftee Indian Village, a replica of a 1750 Cherokee community, is a favorite nearby attraction.

Even with all these activities, the main lobby of the inn bustles with guests playing board games with their children, reading near the fireplace, or just chatting and taking advantage of the warm hospitality of Sue and George Brown.

Cheese Soup

Serves 6

½ cup (1 stick) margarine, melted
1 cloved garlic, crushed or chopped
2 stalks celery, finely chopped
2 carrots, peeled and finely chopped
1 small onion, peeled and finely chopped
1 cup broccoli, chopped
1 cup cauliflower, chopped
½ cup flour
3 cups chicken broth
2½ cups milk
2 cups cheddar cheese, shredded
1½ teaspoons Worcestershire sauce
dash of pepper
salt to taste
¼ cup sliced almonds, toasted

In the top of a double boiler, melt butter and cook vegetables about 5 minutes or until barely tender, stirring frequently. Add flour and stir well. Add chicken broth and bring to a boil, stirring constantly. Add milk, cheese, and seasonings.

Cook 1 hour, covered, in double boiler. To serve, sprinkle with almonds.

Chef's tip: For a heartier soup suitable for a main dish, add cooked ground beef.

Chef's tip: Almost any combination of vegetables can be used in this soup.

Chef's tip: This recipe is easiest with a double boiler. For convenience use the top pan over direct heat in the first steps. To complete the cooking process, put the pan over the bottom pan containing the water.

Chef's tip: This soup keeps well and freezes beautifully.

Celery Casserole

Serves 4 to 6

4 cups celery, sliced
¼ cup (½ stick) butter
¼ cup flour
1½ cups chicken broth
1 cup (½ pint) half-and-half
¾ cup mushrooms, sliced
8-ounce can water chestnuts, sliced
⅓ cup slivered almonds
1 cup bread crumbs, buttered
¼ cup Parmesan cheese, freshly grated

Preheat oven to 350 degrees.

Parboil celery for 5 minutes, drain, and set aside.

Melt butter in a medium saucepan. Add flour, stirring constantly, and cook 1 minute. Add chicken broth slowly, continuing to stir. Bring to a boil and add cream. Pour into a greased 1-quart casserole dish. Add drained celery, mushrooms, water chestnuts, and almonds. Sprinkle buttered bread crumbs over the top, then sprinkle with Parmesan cheese. Bake for 30 minutes until bubbly and light brown. Serve immediately.

Tip: To prepare bread crumbs, melt 1 tablespoon butter and toss with crumbs.

8/4/06 365° is better and less than 20 minutes

Zucchini Muffins

Yields 1½ dozen muffins

Chef's tip: For a loaf instead of muffins, bake in a greased loaf pan, allowing a little additional baking time.

2 eggs
¾ cup sugar
½ cup oil
1¾ cups flour
¾ teaspoon baking soda
¾ teaspoon salt
½ teaspoon cinnamon
½ teaspoon baking powder
1 cup zucchini, grated — 1 fairly small
½ teaspoon vanilla
½ cup pecans or walnuts, chopped
½ cup raisins

Preheat oven to 375 degrees.

Blend eggs, sugar, and oil. In a separate bowl combine flour, baking soda, salt, cinnamon, and baking powder. Add to egg mixture. Add remaining ingredients. Mix well and spoon into well-greased muffin pans. Bake for 20 to 25 minutes or until done.

Gouda Bread

Yields one large, round loaf

Chef's tip: Dough can be divided and baked in two well-greased loaf pans for 45 minutes or until bread sounds hollow when tapped.

Chef's tip: The rosemary gives this bread a lovely aroma.

2 packages dry yeast
5¼ cups all-purpose flour
2 tablespoons sugar
2 teaspoons salt
¼ teaspoon rosemary (optional)
½ cup nonfat dry milk
2 cups very warm water (110 degrees)
2 tablespoons oil
8 ounces Gouda cheese, shredded

Preheat oven to 350 degrees.

Combine dry yeast with 2 cups of the flour, sugar, salt, rosemary, and dry milk. Combine warm water with oil. Add to dry ingredients and mix with electric mixer for 2 minutes.

Add 1 cup flour and mix 1 minute with mixer. Toss cheese with ¼ cup flour and add, mixing well.

With wooden spoon or spatula stir in remaining flour. Mix well. Stir 50 strokes more and cover with towel. Let rise in warm place 45 minutes or until doubled in size. Stir down and beat 20 more strokes.

Put in well-greased, ovenproof bowl and bake for 1 hour. Turn out on wire rack to cool. Slice and serve.

Tip: Be sure to allow plenty of top clearance in the oven. This bread rises over 3 inches while baking.

Grandma June's Baked Tomatoes

Serves 4

3 medium tomatoes, blanched, peeled, seeded, and quartered
1 tablespoon onion, finely chopped
1 tablespoon celery, finely chopped
1 tablespoon green pepper, finely chopped
1 teaspoon sugar
½ cup tomato juice
salt and pepper to taste
1 cup seasoned salad croutons
¼ cup Parmesan cheese, freshly grated
½ cup mozzarella cheese, grated

Chef's tip: If desired, substitute good-quality canned, stewed tomatoes for the fresh tomatoes. Omit onion, celery, green pepper, and tomato juice.

Preheat oven to 350 degrees.

Combine tomatoes with onion, celery, green pepper, sugar, tomato juice, salt, and pepper. Cook over low heat until tomatoes break up. Transfer to a buttered 1-quart casserole dish and mix in ¾ cup of the croutons. Crush remaining croutons, combine with Parmesan cheese, and sprinkle over the top. Bake for 20 minutes.

Sprinkle mozzarella cheese over top, bake an additional 10 minutes, and serve.

Carrot Soufflé

Serves 6 to 8

1 pound carrots, sliced
½ cup (1 stick) butter, melted
½ cup brown sugar
3 tablespoons flour
1 teaspoon baking powder
2 tablespoons dark rum
1 teaspoon vanilla
3 eggs, beaten
salt to taste

Chef's tip: According to taste, up to 1 cup of sugar can be used.

Chef's tip: Substitute 1 teaspoon rum flavoring for dark rum if desired. Omit vanilla.

Preheat oven to 350 degrees.

Cook the carrots in a little water about 15 minutes or until tender. Drain most of water and puree with the butter in a food processor. Add remaining ingredients and mix well. Pour into a well-greased 1-quart baking dish and bake for 45 minutes or until lightly browned and set in the center. Serve immediately.

Tip: A knife inserted in center will come out clean.

Mushroom Business

Serves 8

1 pound mushrooms, sliced
½ cup (1 stick) butter, melted
8 slices bread, cut into sixths
½ cup celery, finely chopped
½ cup onion, finely chopped
½ cup green pepper, finely chopped
½ teaspoon salt
¼ teaspoon pepper
¼ cup mayonnaise
2 eggs, beaten
1½ cups milk
10-ounce can cream of mushroom soup, undiluted
1 cup Swiss cheese, shredded

Sauté mushrooms in 2 tablespoons of butter and set aside. Butter a 2-quart casserole and lay half the bread squares in the bottom, fitting closely. Brush bread with half the remaining butter.

Combine mushrooms with celery, onion, green pepper, and mayonnaise. Spread over bread squares. Cover mixture with another layer of bread and brush with remaining butter.

Combine milk and egg and pour over casserole. Cover and refrigerate several hours or overnight. One hour before serving, spread soup over surface and sprinkle with Swiss cheese.

Preheat oven to 350 degrees.

Bake 45 minutes to 1 hour or until puffed and lightly browned. Serve immediately.

Shoo-Fly Pie

Yields one 8-inch pie

1 8-inch springform pan lined with Foolproof Pie Crust
2/3 cup raisins
1/3 cup molasses
1/4 teaspoon baking soda
1/4 cup hot water
3/4 cup flour
1/2 teaspoon cinnamon
1/4 teaspoon allspice
1/4 teaspoon cloves
1/4 teaspoon ginger
4 tablespoons butter
1/2 cup brown sugar
whipped cream for topping

Preheat oven to 375 degrees.

Sprinkle raisins over bottom of crust. Mix molasses and baking soda with hot water. Pour over raisins.

Combine remaining ingredients with fingers or pastry blender until mixture "crumbles." Sprinkle over pie. Bake for 20 to 25 minutes or until top is lightly browned and filling has set. Cool slightly and remove from pan.

Serve warm with whipped cream.

Note: This is one of those wonderful desserts that fills Fryemont Inn with the aroma of spices while it's baking.

Foolproof Pie Crust

Yields four l-crust pie shells or two 2-crust shells

4 cups flour, sifted
1 3/4 cups shortening
1 tablespoon sugar
2 teaspoons salt
1 tablespoon vinegar
1 egg
1/2 cup water

Mix flour, shortening, sugar, and salt using pastry blender. Combine egg, vinegar, and water and add to flour mixture. Gently mix thoroughly and mold into a ball. Chill 15 minutes. Divide into four portions. Roll out on floured pastry cloth.

Chef's tip: Sue Brown loves this recipe because it makes so much at a time. If you need dough for only one pie shell, put the remaining portions in plastic bags, close tightly, and refrigerate up to one week or freeze up to one month. To use, remove the number of portions needed and allow to come to room temperature before rolling out.

Fryemont Inn
P.O. Box 459
(Fryemont Road)
Bryson City,
North Carolina 28713
704-488-2159

Innkeepers: Sue and George Brown

The Old Edwards Inn
and Central House Restaurant

Some of the most spectacular scenery in North Carolina has to be along the roads leading to the Old Edwards Inn in Highlands. Slicing through every view is one waterfall after another, with names like Bridal Veil Falls, which plunges over the highway. An abundance of lakes and flora, attributed to the high annual rainfall (seventy-nine inches), the highest average precipitation east of the Rockies, adds further to the verdant beauty of this region.

It's easy to see why so many poets and artists have chosen Highlands for their home. Hidden within the tall pines are also the luxurious summer homes of city residents who come to escape the heat in the coolness of Highlands.

Although Highlands' existence is purely accidental—it seems that in the early 1870s, when two men from Kansas were trying to determine a location for their summer resort, they drew lines from Chicago to Savannah and from Baltimore to New Orleans; Highlands is where these two lines intersected—a better choice could hardly have been planned. Their lucky selection became known for its pure air. The first female doctor in the country was the first to prescribe Highlands to patients with upper respiratory problems. Only in recent years has the area seen a great deal of active commercial development, but the older section of town is still sleepy and charming with wonderful shops, including an antiquarian bookstore and hiker's paradise.

The Old Edwards Inn and its innkeepers, Pat and Rip Benton, seem quite at home in this incongruous environment that blends old and new. The wood-framed original structure, completed in 1878 by the Norton family, is now the Central House Restaurant. The name Old Edwards Inn evolved when a Norton daughter married an Edwards, and the Bentons retained the name for continuity. The larger brick portion of the inn, which dates to the 1930s, became the lobby and twenty-one guest rooms. Both were impeccably restored while retaining all the character of the original buildings. The Bentons, who discovered the inn after it had sat vacant for eighteen years, went far beyond the usual measures by matching new wallpapers to faded originals and by having whimsical designs hand-stenciled throughout the inn. The rooms are furnished with antiques from the Bentons' antique shop on Saint Simons Island, Georgia, where they spend the off-season and visit regularly during the season. The recipes used at the Central House Restaurant are first perfected at their restaurant on the island. The fresh seafood dishes were superb; the special Central House Sweet Puppies were like none we had ever tasted, thanks to chefs Susan Anderson and Julie Crisp.

The Bentons simply enjoy the restoration process. Not far from town they recently returned an old ranch house to its former glory. The Home Place, which seemed ideal for large families or small business retreats, is just off the highway leaving Highlands and within full view of Black Mountain. The Bentons have now found and reassembled old, authentic log cabins on the ranch property. With the minimum of modern conveniences, the cabins are for true adventurers or seekers of unusual vacation experiences.

More spectacular scenery greeted our every turn as we took leave. Looking ahead to future tours, we knew no return to North Carolina would be complete without a visit to the Old Edwards Inn and Central House Restaurant, and especially the Bentons—if they stop in the midst of their whirlwind existence long enough for us to catch them.

Tip: Sweet Puppies are a trademark of the Central House Restaurant. They are delicious with everything, even fish.

Chef's tip: A 20-ounce can of canned, sliced apples can be substituted. Four large Granny Smith apples equal approximately 2½ cups.

Chef's tip: This recipe can be varied by adding nuts or other ingredients. For a sweet treat, lightly sprinkle "puppies" with confectioners' sugar just before serving.

Central House Sweet Puppies

Yields 20 to 35 puppies

2½ cups apples, peeled, cored, and chopped
1 cup raisins
3 eggs
1 cup sugar
⅛ cup cinnamon
¾ cup milk
self-rising flour
vegetable oil for deep-frying

Mix all ingredients except flour. Place mixture in a covered plastic container and store in refrigerator until ready to use.

When ready to cook, stir mixture well and add just enough self-rising flour to make a stiff dough. To form "puppies," use a small ice cream scoop to make dough balls and speed up preparation time. Drop into hot oil until golden brown and crisp on the outside. Serve immediately.

North Carolina Mountain Trout
Stuffed with Low Country Crab

Serves 4 to 6

4 to 6 fresh trout, cleaned

Stuffing

⅓ cup margarine
½ cup onion, chopped
⅓ cup celery, chopped
⅓ cup green pepper, chopped
2 cloves garlic, minced
½ cup pimiento, chopped
½ teaspoon seafood seasoning
1 teaspoon salt
½ teaspoon white pepper
1 teaspoon Worcestershire sauce
1 teaspoon horseradish, grated
1 pound picked crab claw meat
2 eggs, lightly beaten
2 cups fresh bread crumbs
2 tablespoons butter or margarine
lemon wedges (optional)

Quickly rinse cavity of trout with cold water, being careful not to wash off the slippery outer liquid from the skin. Set aside in refrigerator, preferably in a slotted or perforated pan with a liner. Cover with ice cubes or chipped ice for the best protection.

To prepare stuffing, melt margarine and lightly sauté onion, celery, and green pepper. Add garlic, pimiento, seasonings, and horseradish to this mixture. Remove from heat and set aside while picking through crabmeat for shells and cartilage.

Place sautéed vegetable mixture in a large bowl and mix in crabmeat. Add eggs and mix well. Then add bread crumbs until mixture holds together well when a small amount of stuffing is pressed into a ball. Correct seasonings if necesssary.

Preheat broiler.

Lay trout on side and, using a tablespoon, gently fill cavity with stuffing. Top each trout with dots of butter and broil about 20 to 30 minutes or until done. To test for doneness, press the skin of the trout—and it should be dry and firm to the touch. Serve immediately with lemon wedges if desired.

Tip: Old Bay is a very good seafood seasoning for adding zip to the stuffing. Be careful not to use too much.

Chef's tip: Lump crabmeat may be substituted, but it is expensive. The claw meat gives the stuffing just as good a taste. Be sure to ask for picked crab.

Chef's tip: This outer liquid is a very valuable moisturizer as the trout is broiling.

Chef's tip: Do not pack stuffing too tightly or fill trout so full that sides bulge.

Tip: We broiled trout on the lower rack due to the lengthy cooking time. They came out perfectly.

Chef's tip: Pat Benton credits a fellow restaurant owner, Florence Anderson, with one of her favorite recipes. She calls it a marvel to work with; it doubles and triples very well. If making a large quantity, use proportionately less green pepper and pimiento. The sauce is so light that it can easily be overpowered.

Chef's tip: Patty shells are preferred at the Old Edwards Inn. Prepared shells can be found in the frozen pastry section of the grocery store.

Flo's Chicken Basque

Serves 4

2 tablespoons butter
3 tablespoons flour
¼ teaspoon salt
pinch of pepper
pinch of nutmeg
1 cup chicken stock
⅓ cup heavy cream
½ cup dry sherry
2 egg yolks, slightly beaten
1 cup cooked chicken, cubed
1 cup cooked ham, cubed
1 pound shrimp, peeled, deveined, and cooked
3-ounce jar pimientos, drained and chopped
1 green pepper, sliced and sautéed until tender
patty shells, toast points, or rice

Melt butter in a medium saucepan. Add flour and seasonings and stir until well blended. Add stock slowly, stirring constantly. Bring to boiling point and boil 2 minutes. Add heavy cream, sherry, and egg yolks. Blend in chicken, ham, shrimp, pimientos, and pepper strips. Heat through and serve in patty shells, on toast points, or over rice.

Central House Bread Pudding
with Rum Sauce

Serves 6 to 8

3 cups milk
2 tablespoons margarine
3 eggs
½ cup sugar
¼ teaspoon salt
¼ teaspoon nutmeg
¼ teaspoon cinnamon
3 cups white bread, cubed
¾ cup raisins

Chef's tip: This great old recipe keeps beautifully in the refrigerator and is almost foolproof.

Sauce

½ cup (1 stick) butter
1 cup sugar
½ cup light cream or half-and-half
¼ cup rum

Chef's tip: Sauce should be milky, not completely clear.

Preheat oven to 350 degrees.

Scald the milk and margarine. In a bowl beat eggs, sugar, salt, and spices together. Gradually add the scalded milk mixture to the egg mixture, stirring constantly.

Mix bread cubes and raisins together in 8-inch square baking pan. Pour milk mixture over bread. Place dish in a larger pan filled about half full with warm water. Bake about 30 minutes or until lightly brown on top and set in the middle.

To prepare sauce, combine butter, sugar, and cream in a saucepan, stirring constantly. Bring just to a boil, lower heat, and stir until sugar is dissolved. Add rum. Serve warm over bread pudding.

The Old Edwards Inn and Central House Restaurant
Main Street
Box 1778
Highlands,
North Carolina 28741
704-526-5036

Innkeepers:
Pat and Rip Benton

High Hampton Inn

Since the early nineteenth century, High Hampton Inn has been a summer retreat, first as a summer home of the aristocratic Hampton family from South Carolina. There as a boy, General Wade Hampton III, the illustrious Confederate officer who later became governor and senator of North Carolina, hunted on these grounds. Then in 1922 the property was acquired from the estate of Hampton's niece, Carolyn Halstead, and her husband by the family of High Hampton's present owner, William McKee.

Nature-lovers, the Halsteads were responsible for planting the famous dahlia garden and the trees that dot the beautifully manicured grounds. The McKee family continues to care for the trees lovingly. A wooden marker placed by each tree makes the identification process an easy one. High Hampton, also a bird-watcher's haven, offers guests the opportunity to spot more than 150 species.

The emphasis here is on natural beauty and relaxing activities. The sprawling main lodge, built with large timbers, chestnut bark siding, and broad porches, is rustic but inviting. Our pine-paneled room, which was spotlessly clean, was simply furnished

and enhanced with colorful hooked rugs made by local craftsmen. In addition to the rooms in the main lodge, there are several cottages available near and along the golf course. The new honeymoon cottage, once a grist mill, has its own lake and boat landing plus fishing gear and a boat.

This "dean" of mountain resorts, part of a 1,200-acre estate, is where people come, generation after generation, to visit with old friends and make new ones. Official host William McKee and his son, Will, the innkeeper, are there to make sure you do just that.

High Hampton offers workshops on art, bridge, quilting, investments, and numerous others. For the sports-minded guest, there is tennis, swimming, fishing, Italian lawn bowling, and archery. For the serious golfer, where else could you play a par 3, 137-yard eighth hole to an island green surrounded by towering trees and mountains? For the younger guests, a flurry of activities during the summer keeps them busy from breakfast to bedtime.

The social hour begins in the late afternoon in the great lobby, where tea and sweets are served. It then moves on to the Rock Mountain Tavern for happy hour and dancing. Dinner is served buffet-style in a gigantic dining hall, usually followed by bingo. The evening we were there, people of all ages were caught up in the game. The guests we met are adamant about High Hampton staying the same in a world that is ever-changing. After one visit, you'll love it. There's nothing else quite like it.

Chef's tip: This dish reheats beautifully and is better the second day. It also freezes well. The inn serves it with roast beef.

Spanish Eggplant

Serves 10

2 large eggplants, peeled and cubed
2 tablespoons butter
1 cup onions, chopped
1 cup green bell peppers, chopped
2 14½-ounce cans stewed tomatoes, drained
½ cup brown sugar
2 tablespoons plus ¼ cup Parmesan cheese, grated
1 teaspoon or more garlic powder
salt and white pepper to taste
1 cup bread crumbs
2 tablespoons butter, melted

Preheat oven to 350 degrees.

Soak eggplant in salted water about 30 minutes. Change water and parboil the eggplant about 30 minutes. Drain and set aside.

Melt butter in sauté pan. Sauté onions and green peppers until done. Set aside.

Combine eggplant and tomatoes. Add brown sugar, 2 tablespoons cheese, garlic powder, salt, and white pepper. Mix thoroughly and add sautéed onions and peppers.

Place mixture in casserole pan. Toss bread crumbs in butter, then sprinkle over eggplant mixture. Top with ¼ cup cheese and bake about 30 minutes or until brown. Serve immediately.

Sunny Silver Pie

Yields two 9-inch pies

½ tablespoon unflavored gelatin
⅓ cup cold water
4 eggs, separated
pinch of salt
3 tablespoons lemon juice
rind of 1 lemon, grated
1 cup sugar
2 9-inch pie shells, baked
1 cup (½ pint) heavy cream

Add gelatin to cold water and set aside to soak. Combine egg yolks, salt, lemon juice, lemon rind, and ½ cup sugar in a rounded-bottom enamel bowl. Set bowl into a larger saucepan of boiling water over high heat. Whip egg mixture until it becomes quite firm and creamy. Then reduce heat and fold in gelatin. Remove from heat but leave bowl in hot water bath.

Beat egg whites until very stiff and add remaining ½ cup sugar. Fold into egg mixture. Divide filling between pie shells and refrigerate pies at least 2 hours.

Whip cream and spread over top of pie just before serving.

Note: This pie is very rich, much like a lemon soufflé. It was the favorite dessert of Mrs. E. L. McKee, William McKee's mother, who along with her husband acquired High Hampton Inn in 1922.

Black-Bottom Pie

Yields one 9-inch pie

Crust

1½ cups (6-ounce package) zwieback crackers, crushed
¼ cup confectioners' sugar
6 tablespoons (¾ stick) butter, melted
1 teaspoon cinnamon

Filling

1 tablespoon unflavored gelatin
½ cup cold water
4 egg yolks, beaten slightly
1 cup sugar
4 teaspoons cornstarch
2 cups milk, scalded
1½ ounces semisweet chocolate, melted
½ teaspoon vanilla
1 teaspoon almond extract
3 egg whites
¼ teaspoon salt
¼ teaspoon cream of tartar
¼ cup sugar
1 cup (½ pint) heavy cream, whipped
2 tablespoons confectioners' sugar

Preheat oven to 325 degrees.

Mix crust ingredients thoroughly and press into 9-inch pie pan. Bake for 15 minutes or until golden brown.

Add gelatin to cold water and set aside to soak.

Combine egg yolks, sugar, and cornstarch. Gradually stir egg mixture into scalded milk, then cook over a pan of boiling hot water until custard coats spoon. Remove 1 cup of custard and combine with chocolate, beating until well blended. Cool. Add vanilla and pour into pie shell.

Add dissolved gelatin to remaining custard. Cool but do not allow to stiffen. Stir in almond extract and set aside.

Beat egg whites and salt until blended. Add cream of tartar and beat until stiff, gradually adding sugar. Fold egg whites into custard and gelatin mixture and pour into pie shell over chocolate layer. Chill until set.

Whip cream with confectioners' sugar. Spread on pie and serve.

Tip: If custard begins to stiffen, beat in 1 tablespoon of milk at a time to keep it smooth.

Layer Cookies

Yields approximately one 10- × 15-inch sheet

Chef's tip: These cookies are served for high tea at the inn. They freeze well.

First layer

½ cup vegetable shortening
1 cup sugar
2 eggs, well beaten
½ teaspoon salt
1 teaspoon vanilla
1½ cups flour
1 teaspoon baking powder

Second layer

1 cup brown sugar
1 teaspoon vanilla
¾ cup nuts, chopped
2 egg whites, beaten to stiff peaks

Preheat oven to 325 degrees.

Cream shortening and sugar, then add eggs. Add salt and vanilla. Sift flour and baking powder together and add to sugar mixture. Mix thoroughly and spread in a greased, medium-size cookie pan.

To prepare second layer, combine brown sugar, vanilla, and chopped nuts. Fold in egg whites and spread over first layer. Bake about 30 minutes or until light brown. Cut into squares and allow to cool.

High Hampton Inn
North Carolina State Highway 107
P.O. Box 338
Cashiers, North Carolina 28717
704-743-2411

Innkeeper: Will McKee

The Greystone Inn

The popularity of the Lake Toxaway area, where the Greystone Inn is located, began in the late 1800s. The rich and famous traveled by trains from the north and by carriages from the south to what was called "Little Switzerland of America." Such notables as Henry Ford, Harvey Firestone, Thomas Edison, and R. J. Reynolds enjoyed the fine food, sports, and dancing to well-known orchestras.

The area flourished, and visitors built summer homes on the lake's shoreline. One of the most impressive was a home built in 1915 for Lucy Armstrong after her first marriage. Concerned for her happiness in such a remote area, her husband encouraged her to spend the summer camping in a tent with her servants before he began construction. Among the comforts she brought from home were fine Oriental rugs, which covered the earthen floors. After her husband's death, she remarried, and the home became known as the Moltz Mansion, named after her second husband. During the Depression she shared her wealth by opening a soup kitchen where she taught young ladies from the country how to cook. At one time, the mansion had five kitchens.

Tim Lovelace, present owner of the Greystone Inn, has created a luxurious, elegant inn where guests can enjoy the mountain scenery and beauty of Lake Toxaway. Careful attention has been given to the furnishings. Thanks to existing photographs, the furnishings have been duplicated with authentic period reproductions and antiques, much like those belonging to Lucy Armstrong Moltz. Each of the twenty rooms in the main inn has a unique personality and is named after a famous individual who summered at the lake when resorts thrived before the great flood of 1916.

Our favorite room was the Ford Sleeping Porch, which is entirely windowed for a magnificent view of the lake.

If you prefer privacy, nothing compares with the historic lakeside cottage, the original guesthouse. A new building, in keeping with the style of the historic inn, has twelve luxury suites on three levels overlooking the lake. Each has a fireplace, wet bar, and jacuzzi. No expense has been spared to assure guest comfort.

There is plenty to do at the Greystone Inn. A trip to Toxaway Falls is a must. Created by the force of the great flood, this is the most spectacular sight in the "Land of the Waterfalls." Along with tennis, golf, fishing, horseback riding, rock climbing, white-water rafting, badminton, croquet, and swimming, the activity most enjoyed by guests is the sunset cruise aboard the twenty-eight-foot *Mountain Lily.*

Lucy Armstrong Moltz would have appreciated the gracious manner in which meals are served at the Greystone Inn. Fine cuisine is served to guests in a glass-enclosed dining room, just a short stroll from guest rooms and suites.

The Greystone Inn has so much to offer that guests return again and again to experience North Carolina hospitality at its very best.

STONE INN

Southern Crab Cakes

Serves 2 to 3

1 egg
2 tablespoons mayonnaise
½ teaspoon dry mustard
⅛ teaspoon cayenne pepper
⅛ teaspoon Tabasco sauce
½ teaspoon salt
½ teaspoon white pepper
1 pound crabmeat, picked to remove shells
3 tablespoons fresh parsley, chopped
1½ tablespoons cracker crumbs
vegetable oil for frying

Tartar Sauce

3 tablespoons dill relish
3 tablespoons onion, minced
1 teaspoon parsley, minced
1 teaspoon lemon juice
3 drops Tabasco sauce
1 cup mayonnaise
1 teaspoon capers, chopped
lemon wedges for garnish

Beat egg, mayonnaise, mustard, cayenne pepper, Tabasco sauce, salt, and pepper until smooth. Add crabmeat, parsley, and cracker crumbs. Stir gently with a fork or spoon. Shape into cakes of desired size and cool in refrigerator for 1 hour or longer.

Heat oil to 375 degrees in a deep fryer or deep skillet. Fry crab cakes for 3 to 4 minutes on each side and drain on paper towels.

To prepare Tartar Sauce, combine all ingredients and mix well. Serve with crab cakes.

Fish Mousse à la Joinville
with Ravigote Sauce

Serves 6

2 pounds raw fish
7 egg whites
3 cups (1½ pints) heavy cream
1 tablespoon salt
6 drops Tabasco sauce
1 tablespoon butter

Tip: We used salmon, which made for a beautiful dish of pale pink and pale green. The inn also uses lobster in this recipe.

Sauce

1½ teaspoons salt
1 teaspoon prepared mustard
2 teaspoons confectioners' sugar
4 egg yolks
½ cup lemon juice
3 cups vegetable oil
chopped parsley, chives, tarragon, shallots, and spinach juice for color

Preheat oven to 350 degrees.

Make sure all ingredients and bowl are very cold. Grind fish into a puree, transfer to cold bowl, and place bowl into crushed ice bath. Fold egg whites into fish one at a time and blend well. Fold in heavy cream a little at a time. Add salt and Tabasco sauce and mix.

Tip: Clean bowl with vinegar and salt before placing in freezer for maximum coldness.

Chef's tip: Fold in eggs slowly using a wooden spoon.

Butter six individual molds or single mold. Pour fish mixture into molds and place molds in pan with 1 inch of warm water. Bake for about 30 minutes or until done. Cool slightly before serving.

To prepare sauce, combine salt, mustard, confectioners' sugar, and egg yolks and blend thoroughly. Add lemon juice and mix well. Begin adding oil slowly, beating constantly. Add herbs and spinach juice for color.

Unmold mousse onto plates. Garnish with sauce and serve.

Fillet of Sole, Bonne Femme

Serves 6

Chef's tip: You can use any fish you prefer.

3 pounds sole fillets
¼ pound mushrooms, sliced
1 bay leaf
2 medium shallots, chopped
1 cup dry white wine
1 cup water
1 tablespoon butter
1 tablespoon flour
4 egg yolks, beaten
2 cups (1 pint) half-and-half
salt and pepper to taste
lemon juice to taste (optional)

Tip: Because sole is such a fragile fish when cooked, we poached it in a large pan that allowed fillets to be laid flat in a single layer. Be careful not to overcook. Use a long spatula to remove fish from liquid.

Cut fillets into desired portions. Heat mushrooms, bayleaf, shallots, wine, and water in pan large enough to lay the fillets flat. Poach about 8 minutes or until done. Remove fish and place in casserole to keep warm. Strain and reserve stock.

Make a paste of butter and flour. Add to stock while whisking rapidly. Bring stock to a boil and whip in egg yolks. Then add half-and-half until sauce is desired thickness. Add salt and pepper to taste and lemon juice if desired. Pour over sole, place in oven for a few minutes to heat, and serve immediately.

Sautéed Pompano Amandine

Serves 4

4 8-ounce pompano fillets
salt and pepper to taste
1 cup (½ pint) half-and-half
1 cup flour
4 tablespoons (½ stick) butter
4 tablespoons oil
½ cup almonds, blanched and sliced
2 lemons, juiced
fresh parsley, chopped

Salt and pepper fillets. Dip in half-and-half and then dredge in flour. Place 2 tablespoons butter and 4 tablespoons oil into sauté pan. Add fish with skin side up. Brown well over medium heat, turn, and brown other side. Transfer to serving plate and keep warm.

In separate pan, melt remaining 2 tablespoons of butter and brown almonds. Add lemon juice. Pour over fish and sprinkle with parsley. Serve immediately.

Tip: If you prefer a lighter lemon taste, you may want to use only one lemon or simply add lemon juice to taste.

Red Snapper Citrus

Serves 4

½ cup onion, finely chopped
½ cup orange juice, strained
2 teaspoons orange rind, finely grated
1 teaspoon salt
4 8- to 10-ounce red snapper fillets
pinch of ground nutmeg
pinch of ground black pepper

Preheat oven to 400 degrees.

Combine onion, orange juice and rind, and salt, and marinate fillets for about 30 minutes. Drain and bake, flesh side up, for about 12 minutes or until done. Serve immediately.

Tip: This recipe is too easy and fresh-tasting to be true.

Tip: Fish will become firm to the touch when done.

Tenderloin of Beef
à la Stroganoff

Serves 8 to 10

4 pounds tenderloin of beef, sliced into ¼-inch strips
6 tablespoons (¾ stick) butter
1 clove garlic, chopped
1 small onion, chopped
¾ pound mushrooms, sliced
7 tablespoons flour
5 bouillon cubes, dissolved in 3 cups water
2 cups (1 pint) sour cream, warmed
1 dill pickle, diced
¼ cup dill pickle juice
1 tablespoon oil
1 teaspoon salt
¼ teaspoon pepper
Accent seasoning (optional)
Worcestershire sauce (optional)
dill weed, chopped
tiny boiled potatoes, rice, or noodles

Melt 4 tablespoons butter in pan or skillet. Add garlic and onion and cook for 2 minutes. Add mushrooms and cook 2 more minutes. Add flour, stirring quickly to make a roux. Add beef stock and boil at least 5 minutes. Remove from heat and add warm sour cream slowly, then add pickles and pickle juice. Keep warm over low heat.

Place 2 remaining tablespoons of butter and the oil in pan. Salt and pepper the beef and sauté. Add Accent or Worcestershire sauce if desired.

Combine sautéed beef and sauce, simmer for a few minutes until heated, and garnish with dill weed. Serve with boiled new potatoes, rice, or noodles.

Tip: The addition of the pickles and pickle may seem strange, but this stroganoff is extremely tasty.

Chef's tip: Add pickle juice to taste.

The Greystone Inn
U.S. Highway 64
P.O. Box 6
Lake Toxaway,
North Carolina 28747
704-966-4700 or
800-824-5766

Innkeeper:
Brien Peterkin

The Inn at Brevard

An antique china cabinet filled with sparkling Waterford crystal and distinctive Beleek china should have been our first clue that Eileen Bourget, innkeeper of the Inn at Brevard, is Irish. Another clue might have been the lacy white curtains at the windows of this charming, turn-of-the-century mansion.

Eileen, a petite and vivacious blonde, was born in County Down, Ireland. When she and her husband, Bertrand, traveled from their home in Rhode Island to search for a place to retire, little did they realize they would purchase an inn.

The Inn at Brevard was originally built as a private residence for William Breese, a well-known attorney and political figure in North Carolina. A reunion in 1911 for the troops who served under Stonewall Jackson was a noteworthy happening at his home.

The Bourgets have transformed the mansion into a bright, impeccably clean inn. There are special rooms, both guest and dining, designed for smokers and nonsmokers. The main building, listed in the National Register of Historic Places, has four spacious rooms and a honeymoon suite for nonsmokers. Most of these accommodations have views down Main Street of Brevard, home of the nationally acclaimed Brevard Music Center.

Determined to guarantee the inn's survival for another century, the innkeepers offer smoking guests rooms in a separate, newer building facing a quiet side street. These rooms feature some elegant Victorian pieces, but the old inn with its hand-carved mantles offers the most interesting furnishings from the period.

Health-conscious Eileen oversees the kitchen, where fried foods are strictly prohibited. Her culinary treasure is Karen Palmer, known by locals as the "Bread Lady." A musician and artist, Karen makes her living baking breads and pastries, which she delivers hot from her ovens to the inn's kitchen door.

The homey atmosphere of the inn is transformed into a more festive one when the season reopens in March (it's closed in January and February) with a dinner dance, quite the social event for Brevard, located in the valley of the French Broad River on the edge of Pisgah National Forest.

Easily accessible from the Blue Ridge Parkway, the Inn at Brevard is a pleasant stopover while touring the "Land of the Waterfalls." You can rest assured the Bourgets will extend a warm welcome.

Tip: This is an easy recipe to increase.

Stuffed Shrimp Beverly

Serves 2 as an entrée, 4 as an appetizer

4 jumbo shrimp, peeled, deveined, and butterflied
1 tablespoon lemon juice
1 tablespoon butter, melted
½ cup ground lamb, cooked and drained
1 stalk celery, diced medium-fine
1 scallion, peeled and diced medium-fine
½ cup plain bread crumbs
1 egg, beaten
curry powder, white pepper, granulated garlic, and celery salt to taste

Tip: Scoring the shrimp with several shallow slits minimizes curling.

Preheat oven to 475 degrees.

Score top of shrimp and place flat, tail down, in baking dish. Combine lemon juice and butter; baste each shrimp.

Combine lamb, celery, scallion, bread crumbs, egg, and seasonings. Mix well, divide into four portions, and place one portion on each shrimp. Bake for 8 to 10 minutes and serve immediately.

Tip: This is an easy recipe to increase and makes a special lunch.

Tuna Benito

Serves 1

1 English muffin, buttered and grilled
4 ounces canned tuna
1 celery stalk, diced
4 parsley sprigs, chopped
2 tablespoons mayonnaise
celery salt, white pepper, and granulated garlic to taste
2 slices tomato, grilled
1 strip bacon, grilled
1 ounce cheddar cheese, grated or sliced
chopped parsley

Preheat broiler.

Mix tuna with celery, parsley, mayonnaise, and seasonings. Spread tuna mixture on grilled muffin and top with tomato slices, bacon, and cheddar cheese. Broil for 3 minutes, sprinkle with parsley, and serve.

Kilarney Cabbage

Serves 4 to 6

1 medium cabbage, cleaned, cored, and chopped into 1-inch pieces
4 strips bacon, diced
1 small onion, sliced
1½ cups chicken stock
½ cup brown sugar
½ cup apple cider vinegar
1 tablespoon granulated garlic
1 tablespoon celery salt
4 dashes Tabasco sauce or to taste

Preheat oven to 350 degrees.

In a large skillet, sauté half the bacon until brown. Add half the cabbage and sauté until transparent. Transfer cabbage mixture to a casserole dish. Repeat this procedure with remaining bacon and cabbage.

In the same skillet, sauté onion until translucent and mix with cabbage in casserole.

Combine chicken stock and brown sugar in a medium saucepan. Bring to a boil and add to cabbage mixture. Add remaining ingredients and mix lightly.

Heat casserole in oven for 10 to 15 minutes or, if casserole is glass, for 2 or 3 minutes in a microwave. Serve immediately.

Chocolate Chess Pie

Yields one 9-inch pie

½ cup (1 stick) butter, softened
3 cups sugar
7 tablespoons cocoa
4 large eggs
12-ounce can evaporated milk
3 teaspoons vanilla
9-inch pie shell, unbaked

Preheat oven to 350 degrees.

Cream butter and sugar. Add cocoa, eggs (one at time), evaporated milk, and vanilla. Mix by hand for 2 minutes. Pour into unbaked pie shell and bake for 40 to 45 minutes or until crust is lightly browned and filling is set. Allow to cool before serving.

Tip: Make sure pie crust is cooled. Otherwise brush with egg white to prevent crust from becoming soggy during baking.

Chef's tip: Do not use mixer.

Tip: To check for doneness, shake pie gently. Pie is done when center is firm.

The Inn at Brevard
410 East Main Street
Brevard, North Carolina
28712
704-884-2105

Innkeepers: Bertrand and Eileen Bourget

The Orchard Inn

Ken and Ann Hough's love of music, good books, and art is what makes the Orchard Inn one of a kind. The Houghs' appreciation of art is reflected in the many paintings and photographs hanging throughout this historic inn. The library, consisting of hundreds of volumes, is housed on two floors. If you decide to curl up with a book in one of the comfortable wingback chairs in the living room, you can relax to the sounds of recorded classical music. Ken, an opera tenor, has been known to join singing guests around the grand piano for an impromptu evening of arias.

The Houghs, originally from South Carolina, first came to North Carolina to honeymoon at a mountain inn. They talked of someday owning an inn. Many years later, in 1981, Ken, headmaster at a Charleston prep school, and Ann, a floral designer, found this mountain retreat, which was built by the Southern Railway Company in the early 1900s.

Ann used her artistic abilities to convert the retreat into an inviting hideaway. Ken, who expected to be only the host-innkeeper, also became the chef by accident. He substituted in the kitchen and discovered a talent he did not know he had. The kitchen is now his domain. The day of our arrival he was busy making peach chutney, so popular it is available for guests to take home.

The Orchard Inn is situated on a 2,500-foot elevation known as the Saluda Rise. The inn offers a panoramic view of the Warrior Mountain Range and surrounding woodlands from a glass-enclosed porch. The same vistas make the airy, colorful rooms on the second floor quite special.

The eighteen acres surrounding the inn are perfect for exploring. There are countless birdhouses plus many trails to hike and streams to see. Ask Ken about his picnics-to-go. He can make your outing even more enjoyable with a variety of menus ranging from a simple hiker's fare to a gourmet feast complete with crystal wine glasses. Dinner is served to guests and to the public by reservation.

The Orchard Inn offers more than gracious accommodations to complement the superb food. There are special weekends with tasty 1,000-calorie-per-day meals for the health-conscious, with brisk walks and hikes on the agenda. Bridge weekends, poetry workshops, mystery weekends, and "Cooking with Ken" classes are also additional inn highlights.

If you prefer solitude, however, pick a rocker or swing on the front porch amid the hanging ferns and pots of bright red geraniums. Or select a rustic twig chair on the deck and watch nature's picture show. The sun disappearing behind the mountains, with the brilliant fall foliage still visible in the shadows, is well worth the trip.

Pâté Maison

Yields three loaf pans

Chef's tip: Chopped fresh garlic can be substituted for granules.

3 pounds chicken livers
1 cup (2 sticks) butter
2 tablespoons garlic granules
2 medium onions, chopped
2 pounds ground pork
1 pound ground veal
¾ cup parsley flakes
2 tablespoons poultry seasoning
¾ cup brandy
4 large eggs, beaten
1 tablespoon salt
½ tablespoon black pepper
4 ounces (½ cup) capers
3 pounds sliced bacon
9 to 12 bay leaves

Preheat oven to 400 degrees.

Sauté liver in half the butter. Add 1 tablespoon garlic granules. Cook liver thoroughly, cool, and chop fine.

Sauté onions in remaining butter and 1 tablespoon garlic granules.

In a large bowl combine liver mixture, onion mixture,

pork, veal, parsley, poultry seasoning, brandy, eggs, salt, pepper, and capers. Mix thoroughly.

Line three loaf pans with bacon, letting strips hang over sides so they can be folded over to cover top. Place 3 or 4 bay leaves in each pan. Fill pans with pâté mixture and fold bacon over top. Place loaf pans in shallow baking pan and fill with 1 inch hot water. Cover with foil and bake 1 hour. Remove foil and cook 15 minutes longer. Let cool, wrap in foil, and store in refrigerator until needed.

Serve in slices about 1 ½ inches thick on a lettuce leaf with a dollop of coarse mustard, a gherkin pickle, and wheat crackers.

Chef's tip: Pâté will keep in refrigerator for about three weeks.

Peach Soup

Serves 6 to 8

8 to 12 fresh peaches (about 5 cups)
1 cup orange juice
1 cup pineapple juice
3 tablespoons sour cream
½ teaspoon ginger, grated
dollop of sour cream and mint leaf or thin slice of peach for garnish

Peel, pit, and slice peaches. Place in blender with orange and pineapple juices, sour cream, and ginger. Blend at high speed for about 15 seconds. Chill and serve with sour cream and mint or peach slice floating on top.

Tomato Herb Soup

Serves 8

Chef's tip: Canned tomatoes can be replaced by 8 to 10 fresh tomatoes, blanched in hot water, peeled, and seeded.

1 large onion, chopped
½ cup (1 stick) butter
½ cup all-purpose flour
2 cups milk
2 cups chicken stock
⅓ cup parsley, chopped
⅓ cup dried basil
2 16-ounce cans tomatoes
46-ounce can tomato juice
salt and pepper to taste
Parmesan cheese, grated

Sauté onion in butter. Add flour, stirring constantly. Cook lightly and slowly add milk, then chicken stock. Add parsley and basil.

In a large stockpot blend roux with tomatoes and tomato juice. Heat to boiling and add salt and pepper to taste.

Serve piping hot with garnish of Parmesan cheese.

Country Rabbit Persillade

Serves 8

5 pounds rabbit, cut up
8-ounce jar Dijon mustard
5 cups chicken stock
1 teaspoon salt
¾ cup fresh parsley, chopped
3 tablespoons garlic, chopped
1 tablespoon red wine vinegar
2 cups (1 pint) heavy cream
chopped parsley for garnish

Chef's tip: Rabbit can often be found in the frozen food section of the grocery store.

Preheat oven to 375 degrees.

Coat each piece of rabbit with Dijon mustard. Combine salt and chicken stock and pour into shallow baking pan. Place rabbit in pan, cover, and cook in oven for 55 minutes.

Drain stock into saucepan. Set aside rabbit but keep warm. Add parsley and garlic to stock. Boil and reduce to a thick residue. Add heavy cream and mix well. Pour cream sauce over rabbit and return to 300-degree oven until ready to serve.

Garnish with chopped parsley and serve.

House Salad Dressing

Yields 5 cups

2½ cups vegetable oil
½ cup vinegar
¾ cup mayonnaise
2-ounce can anchovies
1 tablespoon garlic powder
1 tablespoon Dijon mustard
½ teaspoon salt
½ teaspoon pepper
1½ cups blue cheese, crumbled

Place all ingredients, except ½ cup of the crumbled blue cheese, into a 5-cup blender. Blend at high speed for 15 seconds. Pour into a storage container and add remaining blue cheese. Chill and serve over lettuce or any garden salad.

Chef's tip: Dressing will keep in refrigerator about two weeks. Mix before each use.

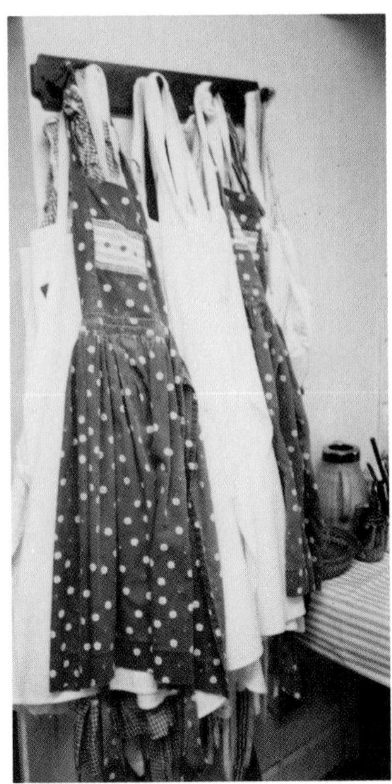

Zucchini and Peas

Serves 6 to 8

6 medium zucchini
2 teaspoons garlic salt
1 large onion
1 tablespoon garlic, chopped
½ cup olive oil
1 cup frozen English peas,
slightly thawed

Chef's tip: This technique "sweats" the bitterness and fluid from the zucchini.

Slice zucchini crosswise in ⅛- to ¼-inch slices. Place on towel or folded cloth. Sprinkle with the garlic salt. Roll in towel and set aside.

Cut onion in half and slice. Sauté with garlic in olive oil until golden. Add zucchini and cook 5 to 8 minutes over high heat. Toss frequently. Reduce heat and add peas. Cook only until peas are heated through and serve before peas lose their bright color.

Raspberry Pie

Yields one 10-inch pie

10-inch unbaked pie shell
¼ cup almonds, sliced
2 pints fresh raspberries
1 cup water
1 cup sugar
3 tablespoons cornstarch
¼ cup (½ stick) butter
1 lemon, juiced
1 cup (½ pint) heavy cream
¼ cup confectioners' sugar

Preheat oven to 375 degrees.

Prepare your favorite pie shell. Sprinkle bottom with sliced almonds. Bake about 10 minutes or until lightly golden. Cool.

Combine half the raspberries, half the water, and sugar in a saucepan. Cook over medium heat and bring to a boil. Mash some of the berries.

Dissolve cornstarch in remaining water and add to raspberry mixture. Return to a slow boil and cook until liquid thickens and turns to a clear, deep raspberry color. Stir in butter and lemon juice and mix thoroughly.

Place remaining raspberries in the cooked pie shell. Pour raspberry filling into shell and set aside to cool.

Whip cream to soft peaks and add confectioners' sugar. Serve pie with a dollop of whipped cream per slice.

The Orchard Inn
U.S. Highway 176
P.O. Box 725
Saluda, North Carolina
28773
704-749-5471

Innkeepers: Ken and Ann Hough

Pine Crest Inn

When driving into the small, picturesque town of Tryon, it would be impossible to overlook the gigantic handcrafted wooden rocking horse standing near the main intersection. Morris the Horse has served as the so-called mascot of this horse-loving town for over sixty years. Morris is more than a landmark. It serves as the community bulletin board where hunt club notices are posted on the saddle. Smaller versions of Morris appear in all the shop windows.

Carter Brown, the first innkeeper of Pine Crest Inn, presumably came to this area in 1917 because of his love of horses. Owner of a successful summer retreat in Michigan, he came to Tryon, situated only one mile from the South Carolina border, because of its location in the thermal belt. The long falls and early springs offered a welcome respite from the bitter Midwest winters.

The pine-paneled main lodge was built in the early 1900s. Brown, who was known for his architectural talents, began to add cottages in the 1920s as more and more guests discovered Tryon, an area first settled by the Cherokee Indians. The cottages were an interesting mix—some stone, some log, some rustic, some modern. All were conveniently located where guests could reach the main lodge by pathways bordered with towering pines. The most unique cottage is the Swayback, a one-room hideaway where F. Scott Fitzgerald is rumored to have stayed. Honeymooners, however, favor the cozy, private, three-room log cabin aptly named the Woodcutter.

The present owner, Bob Johnson, found Pine Crest through a newspaper advertisement when he was a CPA in New Jersey. Bob set many goals for the inn, but the most important one was to introduce innovative menus in the dining room.

Our dining experience at the Pine Crest Inn was memorable. Efficient, attentive waiters, who have been part of the inn's tradition for over thirty years, serve meals in two dining rooms, each with highly polished tables handcrafted of pine and Polomia woods. The flickering lanterns, hunting prints, and heavy oak beams are reminiscent of an English hunting lodge. Recorded classical guitar music adds to the ambiance.

Bob Johnson is committed to maintaining the tradition of gracious innkeeping that Carter Brown began. Residents of this friendly mountain town and guests from all over continue to enjoy the peace and quietude offered by this historic inn.

PINE CREST
INN

Whole Grain Buttermilk Biscuits

Yields twenty 2-inch biscuits

2 cups all-purpose flour, sifted
¼ cup bran
¼ cup oats
1 tablespoon sugar
4 teaspoons baking powder
1 teaspoon salt
3 tablespoons butter
½ cup sour cream
1¼ cups buttermilk

Tip: Start with 1 cup of buttermilk and continue adding more as needed.

Chef's tip: Do not knead, squeeze, or fold dough. This causes the gluten in the flour to make the dough fiberous rather than flaky.

Preheat oven to 450 degrees.

Mix all dry ingredients in a large bowl. Cut in butter, distributing evenly throughout. Drop sour cream into dry ingredients, then start adding buttermilk, turning dough over in bowl until liquid pulls dry ingredients together into a ball. Transfer dough onto a well-floured surface. Roll out to ¾-inch thickness. Cut biscuits with a 2-inch-round cutter or glass dipped in flour. Bake biscuits for 8 minutes at 450 degrees, then reduce heat to 350 degrees and bake 15 minutes more. Serve immediately.

Whole Grain Bread

Yields 4 loaves

2 tablespoons dry yeast
1 tablespoon sugar, dissolved in 1 cup lukewarm water
3 cups warm water
¼ cup blackstrap molasses
½ cup honey
½ cup soy flour
2 cups wheat bran
½ cup ground sesame seeds
½ cup sunflower seeds, coarsely ground
½ cup oats, coarsely ground
½ cup vegetable oil
1½ tablespoons salt
2 cups all-purpose flour
2 cups high-gluten flour
4½ cups whole wheat flour

Chef's tip: This bread is best when recipe is followed exactly.

Chef's tip: Grind seeds in food processor or blender.

Preheat oven to 350 degrees.

Dissolve yeast in sugar water. Add to warm water. Add molasses, honey, soy flour, bran, ground seeds, and oats. Mix well; then add oil and salt. Add flours in order listed until dough is kneadable. Knead vigorously for 8 to 10 minutes, adding flour if necessary, until smooth.

Place dough in an oiled bowl, set in a warm place, and let rise until double. Punch down. Divide into 4 portions. Knead lightly. Roll into tight loaves and place into greased bread pans, patting down flat. Set in a warm place to rise until double in bulk. Bake about 40 minutes or until bottom and sides of loaf feel firm. Slice and serve warm or cold.

Chef's tip: Flour absorbs liquid at a variable rate, so add flour only until dough is kneadable.

Boneless Breast of Chicken Piccata

Serves 2

2 boneless chicken breasts, skinned
flour seasoned with sage, thyme, granulated garlic, salt, and pepper
3 tablespoons clarified butter
3 large cloves garlic, minced
2 tablespoons capers, minced
1 lemon, juiced
¼ cup dry sherry
lemon wedges
fresh parsley, minced

Chef's tip: This recipe is best made for no more than 2 servings at a time.

Tip: To clarify butter, place butter in a saucepan over moderate heat until melted. Reduce heat and skim off any foam. Cook on low heat until milky solids collect on the bottom of pan and liquid is clear. Strain out residue.

Pound chicken to about ¼-inch thickness as evenly as possible. Dredge chicken in seasoned flour. Heat clarified butter and brown chicken breasts on both sides. Add garlic and capers to pan, then quickly dash with lemon juice and sherry. Shake pan to loosen chicken breasts and mix ingredients. Remove chicken from pan and place on platter to stay warm. Reduce remaining liquid slightly, then pour over chicken.

Garnish with parsley and lemon wedges; serve immediately.

Chef's tip: After garlic and capers are added to pan, the liquids must be added quickly as garlic is very easily scorched.

Seafood Fettuccine

Serves 2

Chef's tip: Allow 1 cup uncooked seafood per serving.

2 tablespoons butter
2 cups uncooked, mixed seafood chunks (shrimp, red snapper, scallops)
½ teaspoon salt
½ teaspoon black pepper
½ teaspoon nutmeg
2 teaspoons flour
12 ounces fettuccine, cooked
½ cup heavy cream
¼ cup Parmesan cheese, grated

Chef's tip: Allow 6 ounces (1½ cups loosely packed) of fettuccine per serving.

Chef's tip: Cooked fettuccine can be reheated by dipping into boiling water for 1 minute. Drain well, then transfer to seafood mixture.

Heat butter in sauté pan. Add seafood, salt, pepper, nutmeg, and flour. Stir together for 30 seconds. Add hot fettuccine to seafood mixture. Immediately add heavy cream, stirring constantly until thickened and fettuccine is well coated. Stir in cheese and serve.

Poached King Salmon
with Herb Hollandaise

Serves 4

1½ pounds fresh salmon fillets
2 cups water
2 cups white wine
¼ cup apple cider vinegar
1 unpeeled jumbo onion, quartered
leaves from 1 stalk celery
parsley stems
1 small carrot, sliced
1 teaspoon salt
1 tablespoon pickling spice

Chef's tip: Allow approximately 6 ounces of salmon per person. Pine Crest Inn uses whole fresh King Salmon, which is filleted and skinned for poaching. Any fat can also be removed. Skin is left on for broiling. The bones and head are reserved for making seafood stock for soups and sauces.

Herb Hollandaise

4 egg yolks at room temperature
2 tablespoons lemon juice
¼ teaspoon salt
¼ cup sour cream
2 teaspoons fresh dill, parsley, or lemon basil or any mixture of these herbs
½ cup hot clarified butter

Chef's tip: Herb Hollandaise can be transformed into Mousseline Sauce by folding it into ½ pint of fresh whipped cream.

Tip: To clarify butter, place butter in a saucepan over moderate heat until melted. Reduce heat and skim off any foam. Cook on low heat until milky solids collect on the bottom of pan and liquid is clear. Strain out residue.

Combine all ingredients except salmon. Simmer poaching liquid for 30 minutes to incorporate spice and vegetable essences. Strain through cheesecloth or fine sieve.

Simmer salmon in poaching liquid for 8 to 10 minutes until cooked through but not overcooked. Drain and keep warm.

Chef's tip: Allow 10 to 12 minutes of cooking per inch of thickness at the thickest point of fish. This holds true for any cooking method.

To prepare Herb Hollandaise, place egg yolks, lemon juice, salt, sour cream, and herbs in blender. Blend at high speed for 30 seconds, then start adding hot clarified butter in thin stream. Blend until thick and all butter is used up. Serve immediately over poached salmon.

Chef's tip: This fruit crisp recipe can be used all year long simply by changing the seasonal fruit. Pine Crest Inn uses cranberries and apples at Christmas; strawberries and rhubarb in the spring; blueberries, blackberries, cherries, and peaches in the summer; and apples and pears from autumn into winter.

Fresh Apple Crisp

Serves 12

4 pounds tart cooking apples, peeled, cored, and sliced
1 tablespoon Fruit Fresh
3 cups sugar
½ cup cornstarch
1 tablespoon vanilla
1 tablespoon cinnamon
½ teaspoon nutmeg
pinch of powdered cloves
rind of 1 lemon, grated
juice of 1 lemon

Topping

1 cup (2 sticks) butter, softened
2 cups all-purpose flour
1 cup oats
1 cup bread crumbs
1 cup brown sugar
1 teaspoon salt
freshly whipped cream or vanilla ice cream

Chef's tip: Fruit Fresh keeps fruit from turning dark.

Chef's tip: Pine Crest Inn uses a small kitchen mixer to blend topping ingredients.

Preheat oven to 350 degrees.

Place sliced apples into bowl of water in which Fruit Fresh has been dissolved. Strain. Add sugar, cornstarch, vanilla, spices, lemon rind, and juice and stir. Pour into a 9- × 13-inch pan and bake for 30 minutes.

To prepare topping while apples are baking, combine all topping ingredients in a mixing bowl. Blend until well mixed but crumbly.

Remove apples from oven and crumble topping across apples to completely cover. Return to oven and bake until topping is crisp and golden. Cool slightly and serve while warm with whipped cream or vanilla ice cream.

Brown Sugar Pecan Pie

Yields four 9-inch pies

Tip: This recipe was cut in half with excellent results.

18 eggs at room temperature
4 cups sugar
2 cups brown sugar
2½ teaspoons salt
2 tablespoons vanilla
½ cup blackstrap molasses
½ cup vegetable oil
2½ cups light corn syrup
4 cups pecans, chopped
2 cups pecan halves
4 Flaky Pastry crusts

Preheat oven to 400 degrees.

Break eggs into large mixing bowl. Using large whisk, beat until smooth. Thoroughly mix sugars together in food processor or by sifting and add to egg mixture. Add salt, vanilla, molasses, oil, and corn syrup. Incorporate all ingredients with whisk.

Put 1 cup chopped pecans and ½ cup pecan halves in bottom of each Flaky Pastry crust. Pour filling over pecans, distributing evenly. Bake at 400 for 10 minutes, then reduce heat to 300 degrees and bake 40 more minutes or until set. Cool and serve.

Flaky Pastry

Yields four 9-inch crusts

⅔ cup vegetable shortening
⅓ cup butter, softened
2½ cups all-purpose flour
½ cup whole wheat flour
1 teaspoon salt
ice water

Tip: Take care to add ice water in small amounts until dough ball is formed.

Blend shortening and butter. Sift together flours and salt. Cut shortening mixture into flour mixture. Add ice water until mixture can be formed into a ball that is easily handled. Divide dough into 4 portions and wrap in wax paper. Refrigerate 1 hour before rolling into crusts.

Pine Crest Inn
200 Pine Crest Lane
P.O. Box 1030
Tryon, North Carolina
28782
704-859-9135

Innkeepers: Bob and Diane Johnson

Index

A

B

C

D

E

F

G

H

I

K

L

M

O

P

Q

R

S

T

V

W

Z

A Cook's Tour Notes

HISTORIC NORTH CAROLINA INNS: A Cook's Tour

Typography by G&S Typesetters, Inc., Austin
The book is set in Palatino and Friz Quadrata.

Printing by Hart Graphics, Austin
The text paper is 70 lb. Sequoia matte with 100 lb. Sequoia matte plus lamination for cover. Endpaper is 80 lb. Moisterite matte.

Binding by Ellis Bindery, Dallas

Design and production by Barbara Jezek, Austin
Edited by Alison Tartt, Austin
Photo processing by Davis Black & White, Austin

Cover photograph of quilt by Charles Clemmer
Log Cabin quilt, circa 1860, courtesy of Shumake & Johnson General Store, Mt. Sidney, Virginia